● SCOTCH ●
Its History and Romance

SCOTCH
Its History and Romance

Ross Wilson

Freedom and whisky gang thegither! —
tak aff your dram.

Robert Burns

DAVID & CHARLES : NEWTON ABBOT

0 7153 6091 4

Set in 11 on 13-point Baskerville
and printed in Great Britain
by W J Holman Limited Dawlish Devon
for David & Charles (Holdings) Limited
South Devon House Newton Abbot Devon

Contents

List of Illustrations

Introduction

Inspiring bold John Barleycorn!
What dangers thou canst make us scorn!
Wi' tippeny, we fear nae evil;
Wi' usquabae, we'll face the devil!

So wrote Robbie Burns in his *Tam o' Shanter*. The key word is, of course, *usquabae*—the old name for whisky on the way to its present form. Or, as he wrote in *The Author's Earnest Cry and Prayer:*

But tell me whisky's name in Greek,
And I'll tell the reason.

For the origin of Scotch whisky, like its name, is lost in the mists of antiquity. Uisge beatha was its first recorded name in Gaelic, itself a translation of the Latin aqua vitae, the French eau-de-vie, in English, the water of life. That, the water of life, which the early alchemists thought they had discovered by distilling the essence of grape or grain, is the true and primary meaning of uisge beatha.

There were no grapes in Scotland, but barley abounded in the straths, glens, laichs and fields of Scotland. It was to the barley that the early alchemists in Scotland turned their attention. Exactly when, where or how they discovered that ancient craft of distilling the water of life from the crops around them no one knows, or will ever know. Suffice it to

7

say that they discovered the secret, and today the whole world applauds these pioneers who have made the name and product of Scotland famous.

Was the secret brought by the Scots as they crossed the sea from Ireland and subdued first the Western Isles and then the mainland to which they have now given their name? Was it a secret wrested from the Picts whom they subdued? Did the mystery evolve in an almost haphazard fashion on farm after farm? The possibilities are endless. By degrees it became a normal and natural sideline to farming, as the farmer set aside a portion of his crop to transform it by an inherited and native skill from golden barley into golden uisge beatha.

Today, that water of life flows and flies around the world, bringing its unrivalled comfort, cheer and gladness to millions. From those humble beginnings on croft and farm, uisge beatha, Scotch whisky, has grown to become one of the most widespread and international commodities in the world, so that shipments from Scotland, the only place it can be made, amount to nearly 70 million British proof gallons a year, valued at approaching £230 million ($552 million).*

What is this drink which we have now abbreviated still further into just its geographic adjective, Scotch? Let's leave aside, for the present, the legalities and technicalities. There are time and place enough for them later, but we can examine now the fundamentals of this Scottish mystery.

Like the barley from which it originated, it has grown out of the land of its birth. Like the streams of that land it has flowed through the story of Scotland. The unique, inimitable product of Scotland alone—Scotch whisky is identified with its place of birth and can be made nowhere else—Scotch is a delicately balanced and meticulously prepared combination of the four elements of nature: earth, air, fire and water. To these four elements must be added a fifth: that native,

*Wherever US dollar conversions from pounds sterling are given, these have been based on an exchange rate of £1 = $2.40.

inherited skill to be found in Scotland alone, which results in the balanced combination of the other four elements.

The cunning alchemists of the jagged end of Great Britain have so organised these four elements as to produce the world's premier spirit, and have carried their organising genius to such a pitch that wherever and whenever a man or woman wants whisky it will be there to satisfy their wishes.

But all of this is a long story—as long as that of Scotland itself. And for the moment we must content ourselves with a glance at those four elements so brilliantly combined, arranged and organised into Scotch whisky as the world knows it today.

First, the earth. This yields not only the barley with which it all began—barley in just the strains and qualities demanded by the distiller—but also another indispensable component that goes to the making of Scotch, the peat. Cut from its bogs and mosses, then dried, the peat is fired in kilns, feet under the barley malt after it has completed its controlled artificial germination which begins the conversion of the starch in the grain into sugary materials capable of being fermented. In that peat-drying process a further element of the soil of Scotland is impregnated into the grain to help form the character of the Scotch which will result.

Then the air of Scotland. Not only is it a necessary part of the process of conversion of the grain into Scotch, but it has an importance which cannot be accurately measured, yet which is known as decisive, in maturing the young, ardent spirit into something gracious and mellow, which gives only pleasure to its friends and acquaintances. No artificial aids to speedy maturation are used in Scotland: the bonded warehouses where the spirit grows and matures are bathed only in the pure, cool, damp air of Scotland itself, whether it comes from mountain, plain, ocean or glen.

As early as malting the barley to make it yield a fermentable liquid, during the fermentation of the liquid, worts, into wash, in the years' long maturation of the young whisky into its smooth and polished finished self, in all these, and, indeed, in every stage of the making of Scotch, the fresh Scottish air is allowed unhindered access to that stage of production, whatever it may be.

That third element, fire, is represented in the burning of the peat to impart its distinctively Scottish flavour and aroma to the finished product of Scotland. Other firing methods used in the overall production of Scotch need not necessarily be of Scottish origin, though for long only Scottish coal was used for other firing purposes. But the Scottish element enters in the meticulous accuracy with which that heat is applied. The source of that heat is immaterial; what is important is the degree of accuracy with which it is applied.

Finally, water, maintained by many experts to be of the greatest importance in the four elements. No water in the world is comparable to that used by the Scotch distillers. Many are the tales told about that precious Scottish element. Foreign competitors have even gone to the length of importing water from Scottish lochs and burns, springs and streams, in a vain endeavour to reproduce Scotch in lands far from its place of birth. None have succeeded.

Every Scotch distiller safeguards his water supplies. Every legal safeguard is employed to ensure that the distiller has unhindered and sole control of his water as used in the process. Two stories, for the accuracy of which I can personally vouch, bear this out. Two malt-whisky pot-still distilleries in the Highlands of Scotland, owned by the same family firm who employ the same production methods at their two neighbouring distilleries—they are about a quarter of a mile apart —use water from different sources for such things as mashing the peat-dried barley malt; and they produce two quite distinctive and different malt whiskies!

The same ownership, the same production methods, the same raw materials—except for the water—and yet the merest

10

tyro can distinguish the whiskies from each distillery. What argument can there be about the importance of the water after that?

One more instance—and there are as many as there are distilleries—must suffice. Two malt-whisky pot-still distilleries near another Highland town, under the same ownership but using different water supplies, decided to exchange waters to see what the result would be. Formerly each, using its own supply, produced its own distinctive malt whisky. The exchange was effected: distillery A used distillery B's water, and vice-versa. I quote the actual distiller's report: 'The whisky produced in each distillery during the test, while excellent, was entirely different from that produced before we temporarily inter-changed the waters.'

Such is the mystery of Scotch whisky. A native of Scotland, it can be born nowhere else. It is the very stuff of its native land, of the four elements of Scotland reduced to liquid form by the alchemy of the ages.

It is the Spirit of Scotland. That is no phrase of oratory; no figure of speech. It is indeed the free spirit of Scotland dispensed with true Scottish liberality to all freedom-lovers the world over.

Ross Wilson

Turning Scotch into an Industry

It is one of the ironies of history that the man primarily responsible for turning Scotch into an industry was an Irishman, and a former inspector-general of excise in Ireland at that!

An important official of the British ascendancy in Ireland, Inspector-General of Excise Aeneas Coffey turned inventor, setting his mind to the problem that obsessed many in Western Europe in the latter half of the eighteenth century—the production of a pure spirit in a continuous stream, without, first, the so-called impurities that gave whisky, brandy and rum their individual characteristics, and, secondly, without the time-consuming emptying and re-filling of pot stills and having to double, even treble, distillations.

Coffey was not the first in the field, but he was the most important and successful in the realm of Scotch whisky. Scotch whisky, particularly blended Scotch whisky, would not occupy its present world role without Coffey.

A former veterinary surgeon of Napoleon tried out this continuous distillation idea in London in the 1820s, chiefly at the service of London gin-distillers. Then Robert Stein, a member of a powerful Lowlands whisky-distilling family, was allowed to try out his scheme of a continuous still giving a pure spirit at Attlee's distillery at Wandsworth. That was in 1828 and the following year he tried it out at his brother's

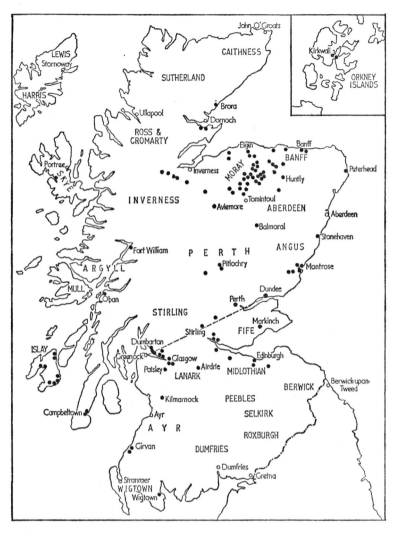

Scotland distils two kinds of whisky: Malt whisky comes from four distinct regions—Highland, Lowland, Islay and Campbeltown. The line from Greenock to Dundee divides the Highland and Lowland whisky areas. Grain whisky has no special geographical links and may be distilled equally on the Cromarty Firth or on the Firth of Clyde. Most of these different whiskies are blended together and bottled in the neighbourhood of Dumbarton, Dundee, Edinburgh, Glasgow, Kilmarnock, Markinch, Paisley and Perth

14

distillery at Kirkliston, near Edinburgh.

The excise officials at the test reported that 'the spirits produced, from the absence of the essential oil, are much more pure and wholesome than those produced by common distillation', adding that 'to separate this oil in the process of distillation has engrossed the attention of many distillers, but hitherto with but little success'.

It was a complicated still in which heated wash was sprayed into a cylinder where it was subjected to live steam to strip it of its alcohol, the spirit vapours passing first to a purifying vessel to collect the heavier impurities, and the pure vapour being condensed later.

The first stills of this kind were erected in Scotland at Kirkliston, a Stein plant, and at Cameron Bridge, a Haig distillery (the Haigs and Steins were related by marriage and descent). The still did not at first meet with the success expected by Robert Stein and in 1830 further experiments were carried out at Haig's distillery at Leith. A number of them were later built at various Lowland sites in Scotland, and the one at Cameron Bridge was still there as late as about 1928.

But it was Coffey's still which ousted all the others and which, though amended and improved, is used today to produce grain whisky in both the Lowlands and Highlands of Scotland. Basically it operates by the continuous stripping of the alcohol, the spirit, out of its surrounding envelope of water by means of the exchange of heat. And where the early Coffey stills at Glasgow and Edinburgh could distil 2,000 gallons of wash an hour to make 200 gallons of spirit, one of the largest in Scotland today can distil 15,000 gallons of wash to make 1,500 gallons of whisky an hour. And if the still can be duplicated, so can the output. One patent-still, or Coffey-still, distillery today, in Edinburgh, can make 16 million gallons of whisky a year.

The original Coffey still is now more often referred to as

the patent still, as Coffey was granted a fourteen-year patent in February 1831, and in October 1832 was given permission to use it for distillation at Dock Distillery, Dublin. Even so, as only a minimum of two distillations had been known until then, he had for years to run his final spirit through a low wines, or spirit, still, to conform with centuries' old practice!

Basically Coffey was an inventive genius, an engineer, a constructor. He did sell one of his stills to a Haig near Dublin. But the Irish distillers, even those like the Jamesons of pure Scottish descent, were too conservative (retrogressive, indeed) to adopt such a new-fangled thing as a still of two columns that did in one continuous process what the pot still had done for centuries in a series of pots and interrupted distillations. Thus Coffey had to move to Britain.

Coffey had set out with the aim of making a 'pure' spirit. Luckily, he did not succeed: his still was not able to produce absolute alcohol, but only a spirit which still had enough congenerics, 'impurities', for it to classify as a whisky, even if of a less pronounced taste, character and aroma than the traditional pot still. As we shall see, it was this very failure to make a 'pure' spirit that was the salvation not only of the still but also of the Coffey-still distillers, the blenders who used the Coffey-still whisky in their blends, and, ultimately, of the whole Scotch whisky industry as we know it today.

A glance at the still and its process is here demanded. Though much enlarged since Coffey's day, the principle remains the same.

Grain whisky, as made in the Coffey, or patent, still, is not made of malt only. It was for various reasons, as we shall see, first made of malted barley and unmalted barley, but today it is made of those two products and maize. Generally the malted barley amounts to about 25 per cent of the cereals mashed. The malt is ground, as usual, and the unmalted grain is first cooked under pressure to burst its starch cells. This allows the excess enzymes in the malt to attack the starch

16

in the unmalted grain during mashing and convert it into saccharine material, just as in the case of the pot-still whisky. It is a prize example of Scottish thrift—making the malt's enzymes work to capacity and convert more starch than that of the barley they come from.

Fermentation is the same as with pot stills, but, of course, on a far greater scale, and for years, luckily well through World War I, the patent-still distilleries of Scotland produced so much yeast that their whisky output was almost a sideline! They still produce commercially viable quantities of carbon dioxide during fermentation, which is then trapped and sold frozen or under pressure. This carbon dioxide business is both profitable and very important to the general economic and industrial wealth of the country.

The fermentation produces wash at these distilleries in a never-ending flow. But instead of being charged into a pot, the wash is pumped to the top of a large column through which it flows in a zig-zag pipe until it reaches the bottom of the column. This one is named the rectifier, and exactly why we shall shortly see.

Almost boiling now, the wash is pumped to the top of the neighbouring column, the analyser. Here it is allowed to fall on to perforated plates and, by means of cups or drip taps at alternate ends of the plates, it is allowed to overflow on to the plate in the chamber below where the perforated plates and the escape cup are repeated.

Meanwhile, steam enters the foot of this analyser column under pressure and as it forces its way upwards through the perforations in the plates—at enough pressure to prevent the wash's falling through the perforations—it strips off the alcohol in the wash lying on the plates and dripping, overflowing, via the cups at alternate ends of the plates. The stripping is logical: alcohol boils, evaporates, at a lower temperature than water; the ascending steam is of a temperature to evaporate the alcohol in the wash, and only spent lees, or wash without

17

spirit, reaches the bottom of the analyser column. In brief, the wash has been analysed.

The alcohol-laden steam finally reaches the top of the analyser column and passes to the foot of the rectifier column, so-called because here the action is, broadly, one of rectification. Here the wash descending the column in its zig-zag pipe is heated by the incoming alcoholic steam, and in return cools, condenses the vapour. Some undesirable elements in the vapour, generally known as fusel oil, are condensed early on; they have a lower boiling point and so condense earlier and are led away to their own receiver. Half-way up the column, the heavier alcohols are checked and drop back through the base to the hot feints' receiver to be pumped continuously to the top of the column and repeat the whole process in pursuit of what pure spirit they possess.

Farther up the column is that calculated point where the whisky the distiller wants meets the right cooling temperature of the incoming wash in its pipes. So here the whisky makes its first condensation on the spirit plate, runs off from the column and is fully and properly condensed. The resulting spirit is a whisky, but a whisky of a slightly higher strength than pot-still whisky—usually under 166.4 proof on the British scale, against 125 proof for pot-still whisky—and without such strong distinguishing characteristics.

The columns of these stills are between forty and fifty feet high, and are subdivided into chambers—with perforated plates of particular importance in the case of the analyser; they are soundly encased in wooden frames, inches thick, to preserve the heat within.

Like pot-still whisky, the patent-still or grain whisky must also be allowed to mature, to develop those characteristics of age and wisdom. This is achieved exactly as in the case of the malt whisky from the pot stills: the new whisky is somewhat reduced in strength, filled into casks, and locked away for years in bonded warehouses where nature takes over and

18

works her miracles.

These two whiskies today combine, blend, to form an admirable partnership: the individualistic pot-still product and the more staid patent-still product. Indeed, it may be said that in accord with the whole tenor of the Scotch whisky industry the blends of today are once again a blend of the ancient and the modern which runs like a golden thread throughout the whole. But, to show the greater activities of the modern (born in 1831!) patent still, it is estimated that the Coffey still of Scotland can produce 116 million gallons of grain whisky a year!

It has not always been so; it was a union slow in coming and then frequently distracted by fundamental differences of opinion. The 'brothers' even fought each other in court, and took, in some cases, opposing sides before a royal commission. That commission attempted and finally brought about a reconciliation so that today all the distillery members of the family live in harmony; they blend and co-operate, though of late the individualistic pot-still whiskies have shown signs of success in making their own way on the markets of the world.

To retrace our steps. The original Coffey-still distillers were aiming, in the then sacred cause of scientific progress, at producing a pure, 'unspoilt' spirit. Particularly the big Lowland distillers of Scotland had in mind the supplying of a 'pure' spirit to the London gin-rectifiers. They naturally used a mixture of malted and unmalted barley in their mash, as was the frequent practice of the Lowland pot-still distillers: there was then a tax on malt. Why pay the tax if the malt is enough to convert unmalted barley as well? The Corn Laws precluded their using imported cereals to any extent, because of the protective tariffs to which they were subjected. And so slow was the acceptance of patent stills in Scotland that in 1837 only just over half a million proof gallons of spirit were made.

In 1846 came the repeal of the Corn Laws which, incidentally, took off most of the import duty on maize, a most valuable cereal whose starch gives a higher alcohol yield than barley. Many were now adventuring with the Coffey still, and in 1847 the patent stills of Scotland made over 2 million gallons of spirit. The boom went on, and by 1857 they were making well over 5 million gallons. That alone gave rise to its own problems: what to do with all this new spirit?

The duty on whisky, still almost all pot-still whisky, was gradually being increased; some of the patent-still distillers disappeared from the scene; others formed an association to agree shares of the market and reduce cut-throat competition. The 1855 Methylation Act allowing 'methylated spirit' to be used free of duty was a slight boon, but the agreements to carve up the market in shares continued, and arrangements were talked about with the English and Irish distillers.

The tax on whisky and other spirits kept creeping up. In 1855 the Scottish duty was equalised with the English at 8s per proof gallon. In 1860 it was increased to 8s 1d and to 10s the proof gallon. Many there were who said such penal, ruinous taxation was the end of whisky!

The tax on malt used in making spirits had been lifted and transferred to the spirits, but even so the government was determined to rob the golden nest of Scotch production/consumption. Consumption went down drastically, but the day was saved by a brilliant young Lowlander, Andrew Usher—he later gave Edinburgh the Usher Hall—who conceived the idea of blending the more expensive malt spirit with the less expensive grain spirit, of blending the pot-still and patent-still whiskies.

He bought up a small pot still near Edinburgh; he already had close connections with famous pot-still distillers whose whiskies he sold wholesale, usually after vatting, or blending several together. What more natural to fight a falling market than to blend not just pot-still malt whiskies but those whiskies with their then Lowland brother, the grain whiskies made by the patent stills?

It has succeeded beyond all expectations, so that in 1972 exports alone of Scotch whisky, 99 per cent blends of malt and grain, or pot and patent whiskies, totalled nearly 70 million British proof gallons valued at close on £230 million ($552 million).

But it was by no means an easy road to success. The indications of the route were there; what was needed was the organising genius of the Scot—here, more particularly, the genius of the Lowland Scot, who is as shrewd and clever a businessman as is to be found, to capture, first, the English market, and finally the world markets. That conquest is still in progress and many battles lie ahead.

Irish whiskey then dominated the whisky market in England, and in Ireland, of course, monopolised the market, just as Scotch whisky, mostly single or blended malt whiskies, did in Scotland. The grain-whisky distillers using patent stills in Scotland continued intermittently for years to form associations to carve up what they considered a restricted market until at last they could stand this temporary uncertain arrangement no longer, and in May 1877 six of them amalgamated to form The Distillers Company Limited of Edinburgh, with a nominal authorised capital of £2 million ($4.8 million), shortly to be reduced to £1 million ($2.4 million). Today their authorised issue capital stands at £200 million ($480 million) and is worth about four times that on the Stock Exchanges, quite apart from other capital at its disposal.

Thus Andrew Usher's initiatory blending of pot- and patent-still whiskies around 1860 and the formation of The Distillers Company Ltd (DCL) in 1877 may be said to have begun the turning of Scotch into an international industry. It was the achievement of individuals, of fiercely independent Scots in an age of fiercely competitive individualism.

21

A few figures of arithmetic to illustrate the initial process: in 1857 about 5.4 million gallons of pot- and patent-still whiskies were made respectively. In 1867, the pots reached 4.8 million gallons, and the patents 5.3 million. In 1877, the pots moved up to 7.2 million gallons and the patents to 11.4 million. The boom had begun.

All booms end in a bust, but in this case the bust did not come until almost the end of 1898. Meanwhile there occurred the greatest boom Scotch had ever experienced. Year after year production and sales of Scotch went on mounting; new distilleries, new firms, were opened, almost overnight. Everyone wanted to 'be in' whisky. Everyone was—to his or her cost.

In fact, Scotch production proceeded so fast that in 1897 almost 14 million gallons of pot-still malt whisky were made, paralleled by well over 17 million gallons of patent-still malt and grain whisky. Scotch was certainly an industry! Even earlier in that decade it had been so acknowledged by a Select Committee of the House of Commons, sitting in 1890-91 to decide whether it was necessary for public health to fix a minimum age of Scotch before it could be sold to the public. Although it did not *have* to be matured, the better firms all matured their Scotch before sale; lesser ones did not bother about such expensive procedures and either sold the whisky hot from the still or at an age of, say, six months or so.

A couple of quotes from the committee put a lot of things in perspective. First, on blending:

Some witnesses desire to define whisky as the spirit made in pot stills, and would deny that name to spirits made in patent stills ... On the other hand, certain distillers in Belfast and Scotland urged that spirits distilled in patent stills from malt and grain were entitled to be considered as whisky; that they are used sometimes as such directly, and are now largely employed in blending pot still whisky. They gave evidence that there was increased demand for whisky of a milder kind, and that blends of pot still and patent still whisky were in large demand by the consumers who thus obtained a cheaper and a milder whisky containing a small quantity of fusel oil and other bye-products.

In fact, the argument had begun whether the patent-still product *was* whisky, but this committee did not attempt to settle that argument. All they would say was:

> Whisky is certainly a product consisting of alcohol and water, with a small quantity of bye-products coming from malt or grain, which give to it a peculiar taste and aroma ... It may be diluted with spirits containing little of the bye-products to suit the pocket and palate of customers, and it still goes by the popular name of whisky. Your Committee are unable to restrict the use of the name ...

On the size of the industry the committee reported:

> The blending or mixing of different kinds of spirits, chiefly whisky, has now become a large trade. From 13 to 14 million gallons are operated upon in warehouses in this way. It is stated that public taste requires whisky of less marked characteristics than formerly, and to gratify this desire various blends are made, either by the mixture of pot still products, or by the addition of silent spirits from the patent stills. In the latter case, cheapness is often the purpose of the blend, but it is also stated that it incorporates the mixture of several whiskies more efficiently ...
>
> Your Committee do not recommend any increased restrictions on blending spirits. The trade has now assumed large proportions, and it is the object of blending to meet the tastes and wants of the public, both in regard to quality and price.

The nineties were certainly Scotch's first boom period, when the old craft reached the level of a really important industry: gone were the days of the peasant distiller, the small-time merchant.

After this select committee report, production in Scotland went on thus: in 1896-7, it amounted to 28.5 million proof gallons; in 1897-8, to 33.7 million; in 1898-9, to 35,769,000 gallons; and then it fell to 31,798,000 in 1899-1900. Thereafter it continued falling for the next few years.

Distilleries multiplied until they totalled 161 in 1898-9, their peak year, never since rivalled. Stocks of Scotch mounted similarly, from 77 million gallons in 1896-7 to 110 million in 1899-1900, and continued climbing until they reached 121,778,0000 gallons in 1904-5.

Home consumption kept pace in the nineties with that production and increase in stocks. In the 1860s, Scotch consumption was almost entirely confined to Scotland and was around the 10 million gallons a year mark; trade with England and abroad was very small. In the 1870s and 1880s it gradually increased as the Scots penetrated the English market, but total UK consumption was still under 20 million gallons a year. It only passed that level in about 1890, and by the middle of the decade was around the 21 million mark. By 1899-1900 it reached 25 million gallons and the following year just passed that mark to total 25,241,000 gallons. That was UK consumption alone, and thereafter a decline set in because of adverse economic conditions at home.

The catastrophic event that shook the whole industry was the Pattison failure of late 1898. Pattisons' was certainly the most well advertised blending firm and considered the top middle-man between distillers and the public. Actually, the firm had many rivals, more discreet and financially sound men whose businesses persist today, but the Pattisons were symbolic of Scotch as an industry that everyone had to 'be in'. Theirs was, in brief, a case of over-spending and under-capitalisation; of reliance on the investing public without comparable business ability. The two brothers received gaol sentences.

The Pattison failure hit the banks hard, as well as many members of the investing public. More important, it reverberated through the industry for a generation or more and its full and final effects can be observed in the caution of the industry even today.

That, the minor increases in duty since Gladstone had raised the duty in 1860 to the 'staggering' 10s a proof gallon, and the natural adventurousness of the Scots—remember, Scotch had been an export since it had been smuggled out of the Highlands and its other illicit stills—combined with the signs of a shrinking home market to push up exports to what was considered the surprisingly high figure of 5 million gallons a year in 1900.

In the UK recession of ensuing years, those exports went ahead faster than ever, there were ample stocks, the home market was no longer expanding, and director after director went abroad to find markets for his product, first to the colonies and those regions ruled by British military forces, and then to the USA. So diligent were their efforts, so good their product, that by 1908 they had lifted their exports from the 5 million gallons of 1900 to 8 million gallons. The Lloyd George budget of 1909-10—it was so revolutionary that it took a year to pass—increased the tax on Scotch by about one-third, moving it up from the 11s a gallon it had reached during the Boer War to 14s 9d a proof gallon, and added yet another export impetus.

Before that budget Scotch had been slipping at home because of the poor economic climate; on the eve of the budget it was just about to recover, or at least showing signs of recovery. Once again it slipped back into the slough of tax despond on the home front and, conversely (naturally, if you will), forged ahead even farther on the export front, so that on the eve of the outbreak of World War I Scotch exports just passed the 10 million gallons mark. That was higher than they ever attained until the calendar year 1940 when exports amounted to more than 11 million gallons. And that total was largely achieved by the American importers' stockpiling in case of further war disasters and shortage of supplies. In the financial year on the eve of the war, 1938-9, Scotch exports totalled 7.7 million gallons, less even than in the year before the outbreak of World War I.

The Lloyd George budget of 1909-10 coincided with a famous decision given by a royal commission which settled what Scotch whisky was, and 'legitimised' grain whisky as made in the patent still. The details of that commission and events leading up to it will be detailed later; their definition is the important matter. Realising the importance of Scotch as an industry, the commission issued an interim report in June 1908, after twenty-two sittings, examining seventy-seven witnesses, and visiting some distilleries. That interim report made these two recommendations:

1. That no restrictions should be placed upon the processes of, or apparatus used in, the distillation of any spirit to which the term 'whiskey' [their consistent spelling] may be applied as a trade description.

2. That the term 'whiskey' having been recognised in the past as applicable to a potable spirit manufactured from (1) malt, or (2) malt and unmalted barley or other cereals, the application of the term 'whiskey' should not be denied to the product manufactured from such materials.

So important was Scotch as an industry, so valuable its role in the national economy, that a year later, in July 1909, the commission issued its final report with its definition of Scotch whisky which remained of legal precedent value until its incorporation, with additions, in the Finance Act of 1933, and its consolidation into statute law in 1952.

That definition was given in this paragraph:

Our general conclusion, therefore, on this part of our inquiry is that 'whiskey' is a spirit obtained by distillation from a mash of cereal grains saccharified by the diastase of malt; and that 'Scotch whiskey' is whiskey, as above defined, distilled in Scotland; and that 'Irish whiskey' is whiskey, as above defined, distilled in Ireland.

The whole of Ireland was then, of course, part of the United Kingdom. But not only did this definition, later adopted into law, make valid the patent still and its spirit as part and parcel of the Scotch whisky industry; more important it gave a geographical significance and interpretation to the adjective 'Scotch'. That has been of the greatest importance, especially with its incorporation into Statute Law and its acceptance by other nations as defining Scotch whisky, in the industry's never-ending pursuit and prosecution of bogus 'Scotches' around the world. Scotch whisky can be made only in Scotland. And that geographic interpretation of 'Scotch' is not solely a protection of a valuable national asset —responsible for earning millions of pounds sterling annually in foreign currency—it is also the ground of an intensive consumer-protection campaign, so that the man (or woman) asking for Scotch will receive the product requested.

Like any other industry of comparable size in the years before, during and after World War I, the Scotch industry was also the scene of many amalgamations and takeovers. These need not delay us here; they are too many to list and some of the partnerships which evolved will be apparent in the appendices to this volume. But their very magnitude and occurrence indicate the major industrial status assumed by this former peasant-gentleman-smuggler occupation; the product of the glens of Scotland had now become the subject of the Stock Exchanges first of the United Kingdom and then of the English-speaking world. Later, it was to become even more international.

Before leaving that 1908-9 royal commission we may also note their report on compulsory maturing of Scotch. In the final report the commissioners quoted the 1890-91 select committee that 'compulsory bonding of all spirits for a certain period is unnecessary and would harass trade'. Further, that 'the testimony was practically unanimous that compulsory bonding would harass trade, and was altogether unnecessary'. With that the royal commission agreed. The royal commission added that 'a system of compulsory bonding would necessitate additional warehouse accommodation, and that the provision of such accommodation would throw considerable expense upon some of the pot-still distillers and the majority of the patent still distillers'.

Such compulsory bonding, they thought, 'could only be

27

justified if it were established that such a restriction of trade is necessary in the interest of public health'. Discussing the evidence and their own findings, the commission concluded that 'it is not desirable to require a minimum period during which spirits should be matured in bond'.

So it remained until World War I, when, among other schemes, Lloyd George had ideas of taxing Scotch at double the rate, then of outlawing it, then of Prohibition. Finally, James (later Lord) Stevenson talked him out of these harebrained notions and persuaded him to pass an act, in 1915, requiring that Scotch and some other spirits must be matured for a minimum of three years. Such was now the importance of Scotch whisky as an industry that within a year of the war breaking out it had become the subject of an Act of Parliament making lengthy maturing legally compulsory! That war saw the Scotch industry, particularly its patent-still distilleries, achieve national status on the grand scale.

The Coffey-, or patent-, still distillers had always been great producers of yeast. With the outbreak of war in 1914, foreign yeast supplies were cut off. But for the natural production of yeast in the course of making patent-still whisky, so recently fully legitimised, the nation and its Forces would have been without yeast and so without bread etc for the duration.

As important, if not even more so, the patent-still distillers made a direct contribution to the mechanism of winning the war. These distilleries were able to produce a very high strength spirit, higher in proof strength than that required to make grain whisky. Little by little their entire output of spirit was given over to high strength spirit absolutely vital to making explosives. Moreover, the patent-still output was also diverted to making chloroform and other anaesthetics, and even its bye-product, fusel oil, was invaluable in coating the wings of the nation's aeroplanes.

In all, the Scotch distillers contributed over 30 million proof gallons of high grade spirit to the British and Allied war effort, a contribution without which the war could not have been won. In late 1916, with the growing need for acetone as a vital material for the production of high explosives to ensure victory, three major Scotch grain whisky distilleries were converted to manufacture acetone, a production actually in process when the US entry into the war made further production unnecessary. But such was the sheer technical ability, the undaunted patriotism of the Scotch distillers, that had it been necessary they would have produced acetone as an additional and essential war material.

No greater industrial and national status can be claimed for any industry than that it plays a vital part in ensuring national survival at a time of war. The Scotch whisky industry achieved that level of national grandeur in the nation's hour of peril, in World War I.

🏺 2 🏺

The Romance of Scotch Whisky

O Caledonia! stern and wild,
Meet nurse for a poetic child!
Land of brown heath and shaggy wood,
Land of the mountain and the flood . . .
                                    Sir Walter Scott

There is the very stuff of the romance of Scotch whisky: that the essential, distilled spirit of the land, *Ultima Thule* of Virgil, which flows its turbulent yet tranquillising course through all the riotous story of the land, should now penetrate every free corner of the civilised globe—and even seep through the Iron and Bamboo Curtains—accepted everywhere as the premier potable spirit of the world.

That *is* romance: that the sideline of the peasant farmer, of the clan chief in his stronghold, should now after all these centuries be the drink of royalty, wealth and excellence wherever men and women are free.

That *is* romance: that this contemptuously disregarded land's end should become the sole source of the world's supreme beverage spirit. It is no good luck story: it is all due to the native ability of the land's inhabitants. How it all began is anybody's guess. Did the Scots bring with them the secret of distilling uisge beatha when they crossed over from Ireland to the Mull of Kintyre, just across the sea from them? And then spread up along the Western Isles and along the south-west to north-east geological structure of the country until they and their skill arrived in the north-east of Scotland, today the prime centre of that ancient pot-still distilling craft? Did the skill cross the North Sea from the Netherlands to the eastern coast of Scotland and penetrate inland? Was it simply the 'accidental' discovery of the first natives of that land?—discovered as they dried their grain by means of their native fuel, peat, and attempted, in folklore fashion, to extract the divine, the immanent spirit of life in the barley?

We shall never know with any certainty. Accidents never happen in history, coincidences often, and the native genius of the people may well have discovered this secret of extracting the water of life from their native grain by trial and error while in search of the life within the barley.

Recording the long, historical legend of whisky in his *Heather Ale—A Galloway Legend*, Robert Louis Stevenson added a note to the poem: 'It is needless to remind the reader that the Picts were never exterminated, and form to this day a large proportion of the folk of Scotland ... possibly also the distillers of some forgotten spirit.'

Why should every skill, every discovery, be attributed to an outside source, be considered an importation? Though certainly the theory that the art of extracting the water of life from the barley by means of distillation arrived when the Scots crossed the sea to nearby Kintyre and the Hebrides has much to commend it.

The geological-geographical structure of Scotland, its ranges of mountain peaks and glens between them, runs from the south-west to north-east, and for centuries the secret art of making uisge beatha was confined to the Hebrides to the west and beyond the Grampians to the north as the craft moved up along the glens to its final full flowering in Speyside, only gradually overflowing into the central belt of the Lowlands of Scotland.

It was not an age for recording in detail the ordinary, everyday normal processes and activities of life and living such as obsesses the Western world today. Maybe the monks contributed their share to the ancient craft. They were skilled craftsmen in many directions and many and varied were the contributions they made to the growth of our culture and science. So it comes as no real surprise to learn that the earliest record we have of uisge beatha—aqua vitae in official terminology—occurs in the Scottish Exchequer Rolls for 1494 where there is this entry: 'To Friar John Cor, by order of the King, to make aquavitae, viii bolls of malt.' (A boll was an old Scottish measure of six bushels or under.)

Three things are noteworthy: it was a monastic distillation, under royal patronage, in the capital of Scotland—a capital in the Lowlands. The local drink of the people was already coming from the country to the capital, to the table of the king—and, ominously, was under government control.

Already it was a royal drink. For instance, the accounts of the Lord High Treasurer of Scotland, 1498: 'Item: to the barbour that brocht aquavite to the king in Dundee be the Kingis command—ix shillings.'

Again, when King James IV was in Inverness during September 1506, the treasurer's accounts have entries for the 15th and 17th of the month respectively: 'For aqua vite to the King—iiis', and 'For ane flacat of aqua vite to the King—vs.'

The court, of course, adopted the language of international culture and diplomacy, Latin, not the tongue of the masses— the Gaelic, with its name of uisge beatha. They meant the same—the water of life.

The reference to the 'barbour' (barber) and the king's 'aqua vitae' at Inverness is of interest. The barbers were the precursors of the surgeons and in 1505 James IV, with that fatal Stuart bent to monopolies, granted to the surgeon-barbers of Edinburgh the rights of bodies for dissection and an associated monopoly of making and selling aqua vitae within the city: associated, because of the alleged medicinal qualities of aqua

Page 33 (above) 'A Highland Whisky Still'—engraving after a painting by Sir Edwin Landseer, 1829; *(below)* 'The Jolly Beggars'—engraving by J. M. Wright

Page 34 (above) A Scottish inn, c 1800; (below) Festival of the Highland Society of London—the health of the Queen, with 'Highland Honours'

vitae, the elixir of life given by God in the later days of man!

All the world hates a monopoly, and it is no surprise that a good woman, Besse Campbell—her very name implies the western origin of uisge beatha-distilling in Scotland—tried to break the monoply some fifty years later and the Bailies of Edinburgh 'ordained Besse Campbell to desist and ceis from making aqua vitae within the burgh in time coming' unless she had the barbers' permission to do so. History does not relate whether she paid the barbers for the privilege (a common solution to monopolies), moved out of the burgh, or carried on regardless.

It was not a documenting age, but an act of the Scottish Parliament of 1555, forbidding the export of victuals generally in a time of famine, made this exception: 'It salbe leiffull to the inhabitants of the burrowis of Air, Irvin, Glasgow, Dumbertane and uthers [Ayr, Irvine, Dumbarton] our Soverane Ladys liegis dwelland at the west setis to have [send] bakin breid, browin aill and aqua vite to the Ilis to bertour with uther merchandice.'

That same century saw also the best eulogy penned of uisge beatha. It comes from Holinshed's *Chronicles of England, Scotland and Ireland*, published in 1578, the Scottish account being lifted from the *Scotorum historiae* of Hector Boece, published in 1527. Shakespeare used Holinshed extensively for his *Macbeth*, but, most curiously, omitted this passage from Holinshed concerning uisge beatha:

Beying moderatelie taken, it sloweth age, it strengtheneth youthe; it helpeth digestion; it cutteth fleume; it abandoneth melancholie; it relisheth the harte; it lighteneth the mynde; it quickeneth the spirites; it cureth the hydropsie; it healeth the strangury; it pounceth the stone; it repelleth grauel; it puffeth awaie ventosite; it kepyth and preserveth the head from whyrling—the eyes from dazelyng—the tongue from lispyng—the mouth from snafflyng—the teethe from chatteryng—the throte from ratlyng—the weasan from stieflyng—the stomach from wamblyng—the harte from swellyng—the bellie from wirtch-

35

yng—the guts from rumblyng—the hands from shiueryng—the sinowes from shrinkyng—the veynes from crumplyng—the bones from soakyng... trulie it is a soueraigne liquor.

'Truly, it is a sovereign liquor...' Such has it remained to this day, as well the world testifies by increasing sales each year, by drinking it in larger and larger quantities each and every year, if not from China to Peru, at least from Hong Kong to Peru!

Holinshed refers, too, to the three versions of uisge beatha —simplex, composita, and perfectissima—and Darnley, the second husband of Mary, Queen of Scots, intoxicated a French visitor to the court on composita, the first specific mention of the effects uisge beatha could produce. These three classifications in Latin terminology correspond with the three classifications given us by Fynes Moryson, a writer of guide-books, tourist literature and pseudo-solemn works in the later years of Queen Elizabeth I of England. Fynes Moryson tells us that three kinds of spirit were known in the isles, and were graded by the distillation process itself and the quality of the resulting drink: they were *usquebaug*, *testarig*, and *usquebaug-baul*. The simplex, or *usquebaug* (or *usquebaugh*), was distilled twice; the composita, or *testarig* (or *trestarig*), was distilled three times; the perfectissima, or *usquebaug-baul* (or *usquebaugh-baul*) was distilled four times and reported so strong that two spoonfuls were alleged to endanger a man's life! Their modern successor, uisge beatha, or Scotch whisky, has been so perfected in its distillation that it needs no more than two distillations.

In fact, the more malt used, the nearer to perfectissima— unmalted barley was frequently added to the malt in the mash—and an Act of 1579 'Anent the making of aquavitie' shows not only the increasing use of malt and the expansion of the industry among households but what may now be termed a text-book example of class legislation. For the Act said: 'Undirstanding that thair is ane greit quantitie of malt consumit in the haill partis of this realme be making of aquavitie quhilk is ane greit occasioune of the derth within the samin', the brewing and distilling of aquavitie was forbidden from 1 December following until 1 October 1580—the normal date of the beginning of a harvest—except to noblemen, barons, and gentlemen who could brew and distil from their own malt for their own and their friends' use.

To cite but a very few of the references to Scotch in the years following, illustrating its normal place in the heritage of Scottish life and living, we have, for instance, the account in the register of the privy council of distilling in a private house in the parish of Gamrie, in Banffshire, in 1614, when a man was accused of breaking into the house, committing an assault and knocking over some 'aquavitie'.

As early as 1618 is one of the earliest references to 'uiskie' as drunk at the funeral of a Highland laird. An unpublished letter of February 1622, by Sir Duncan Campbell of Glenorchy to the Earl of Mar, recounts that certain officers sent by the king had been given the best entertainment that season and the country allowed—'For they wantit not wine or aquavite.' In short, locally made whisky.

It was not long before whisky took the stage in the Civil War, as a weapon in the fight between king and Parliament. In England the parliamentarians imposed the Dutch import of excise duty on 'Strong Waters' and aqua vitae, imported or domestically made, in 1643. Scotland was not then subject to Westminster but the following year the rebel Scots took a leaf out of the Londoners' book and by an Act of Excyse imposed a duty of 2s 8d 'one everie pynt of aquavytie or strong watteris sold within the country'. Then, 34 Scottish pints equalled about 12 English gallons, so the rate of duty was some 7s 6d per English gallon. At least the excise was a tax only on the bulk, the quantity; they had not then got around to measuring strength and taxing according to that.

The collection of the tax was, however, very haphazard:

how could it be otherwise with whisky-distilling a private farm industry of the home for the main part? There were no roads in the depths of the Highlands; there was no army of tax collectors. There is the case of Robert Haig, who had settled at Throsk in the parish of St Ninian's, Stirlingshire, and distilled on his own farm. He is typical of thousands, but for one unfortunate occurrence—of working his still on the Sabbath! An entry in the Kirk Session Record of St Ninian's Parish Church for 4 January 1655 explains it all:

> Compeared Robert Haig being summoned for Sabbath breaking and Wm Reid, John Groby, William Harley and Christian Eason, Witnesses. Robert Haig denied he knew any such thing as was laid to his chairge. The witnesses deponed unanimously that they saw the caldron on the fyre, and a stand reiking and that they heard the goodwife say 'the lasse has put on the caldron and played some after-wort' and she knew not whether her caldron was befor on the fyre on a Sabbath day and had she been at home it should not have been done (for she was byt presentlie cam'd from Alloway Church). So it being only some pynts of small drink played by a servant lass naither maister nor mistresse accessarie to it upon engadgment of Christian carriage for the future, rebuked before the Session.

Came the Stuart Restoration and the imposition of the excise by means of a parliamentary statute signed by the king. But this by no means interfered with the normal and occasional distilling carried on as a sideline to farming. In some cases, a burgh or a shire might be taxed for an estimated amount of whisky made, but more often at this stage it was duty free. How else could it be, considering the geography of the country? 'Caledonia, stern and wild...'

Or consider the case of Duncan Forbes of Culloden, the Whig jurist and politician who sided with the revolutionaries who supplanted James VII and II by William and Mary, and 'suffered the loss of his brewery of aqua vitae by fire in his absence'. This was Ferintosh, the 'ancient brewery of aquavity in Cromarty'. It is the first mention of a famous individual whisky.

As Forsyth put it in his *Beauties of Scotland* (1805):

The small village of Fairntosh [Ferintosh, Ross-shire] only deserves notice on account of a singular privilege which its proprietor, Forbes of Culloden, long enjoyed. At the time of the revolution, in 1688, Mr Forbes of Culloden was a zealous Whig, in consequence of which his estates were laid waste, particularly the barony of Fairntosh, on which extensive distilleries belonging to him were destroyed. As a compensation, the parliament of Scotland granted to him, in 1690, freedom from excise for these lands, on condition that he should make an annual payment of 400 merks Scots...

The concession was later amended and finally, in 1784, with Pitt's reforms, withdrawn completely. The laird did, however, receive *some* compensation—£21,000.

Ferintosh is, perhaps, more widely known generally today because of Burns's lament on the withdrawal of Forbes's privilege:

> Thee Ferintosh! O sadly lost!
> Scotland lament frae coast to coast!
> Now colic grips, an' barkin hoast,   [cough]
>   May kill us a';
> For loyal Forbes' charter'd boast
>   Is ta'en awa!

To revert to the Restoration period, the excise on aqua vitae made in Scotland was ended. Imported liquors were taxed, if they did not escape by smuggling, and in all a sum of money was collected from each shire and burgh to help in the accumulation of the £(Scots) 440,000 paid each year to the king. If the levies fell below the quota in any district, the difference was made up by a tax on malt. In 1681 the malt tax was made general and in 1693 was ended the exemption of the tax on aqua vitae and a general duty of 2s a pint was imposed. Two years later the malt tax was removed—but the duty was increased by threepence a pint.

However, distilling malt whisky, sometimes varied by the addition of a portion of unmalted barley to the malt itself and then usually called grain whisky, continued as basically a domestic practice: it would be too ambitious to call it a domestic industry. It was a widespread practice, though tuppeny ale was the greatest volume beverage, while the better-off drank claret—often to excess—and brandy from France, preferably smuggled.

A few public distilleries were set up, and in 1707 came the Act of Union binding Scotland and England into one nation and assimilating the spirit duties in the two lands in amount, mode of collection and revenue assessment. In brief, the hated excise. From 1709 to 1742 duty on whisky was 3d and 6d a gallon, and during the English gin crisis, when the Prohibition-trend Act of 1736 was passed—the Anti-Gin Act—Scotch whisky was exempted, as it was again when the act was repealed and replaced by a saner one in 1743. In the event, then, the Scottish and English spirit duties were distinct and different until the unification of 1855.

The French attempted—and failed—to invade Scotland on behalf of the exiled Stuarts, and roads were built in the Highlands. Meant to ensure strict military control, the roads had also the effect of encouraging the export of Highland malt whisky to the Lowlands—so long, then, has Scotch been an export.

General Wade was the great road-builder, commemorated in particular by an obelisk on the road between Inverness and Inverary:

> Had you seen these roads before they were made,
> You would lift up your hands and bless General Wade.

On the general's staff was a Captain Edward Burt whose published *Letters* refer to the abundance of claret and brandy among the upper classes, but nevertheless give the palm to Scotch: "The glory of the country was Usky,' wrote the captain. That opinion is as true today as when penned.

In 1716 Martin published his *Account of the Western Isles*, and, in effect, cribbed from Fynes Moryson's description of

40

'common usquebaugh, another called trestarig, *id est*, aqua-vitae, three times distilled, which is strong and hot; a third is four times distilled, and this by the natives is called usque-baugh-baul, *id est*, usquebaugh, which at first taste affects all the members of the body ...'

So native a spirit was the Scottish uisge beatha that during the gin crisis in England when a 'temperance' reformer pointed to the strong healthy Highlanders as prime examples of water-drinkers uncorrupted by gin, one of the hated and despised excise officers in Scotland wrote in angry reply: 'The ruddy complexions, nimbleness, and strength of these people is not owing to water-drinking, but to the aqua vitae, a malt spirit which is commonly used in that country, which serves for both victual and drink.'

One of the 'blessings' brought by the 1707 Act of Union was the introduction of the English malt tax, though at only half the English rate. Apart from the riots occasioned by that tax, that and the duty of the aqua had the effect of beginning to turn distilling into an industry and, more important even, of initiating widespread and intensive illicit distillation. The Scots, in effect, were reacting in individualist fashion: these taxations were nothing, in their opinion, but an unwarranted invasion of personal rights and liberties. And as government control and taxation tightened during the eighteenth century, so developed together these twin phenomena of industrialisa-tion and illicit distilling until almost a state of undeclared civil war came into being.

Then came the tragedy of the '45, Bonnie Prince Charlie's ill-fated attempt to regain the throne and kingdom for the Stuarts ... Whisky played its part even in the bloody slaughter committed by Cumberland, the Butcher of Culloden. For *The Journal of Bishop Forbes* reports that 'Mr John Mait-land, chirurgeon for the soule ... a Presbyter of the Episcopal church of Scotland ... was attached to Lord Ogilvie's regi-ment in the service of Prince Charles, 1745. He administered

Holy Eucharist on the Culloden field, it is said, with oat cake and whisky, the requisite elements not being attainable ...'

The '45 was followed by the greatest spate of road-building ever witnessed in the Highlands, an achievement as beneficial to Highland malt whisky, in fact, as was the nineteenth-century railway boom in bringing the whisky of that region to the south. Not that the southern part of Scotland was lacking in its own whisky production; Arnott's *History of Edinburgh* tells us that in 1777 there were only eight licensed stills in the city against some 400 unlicensed stills. But by then industrialisation was setting in, with several big, professional distillers making spirit for the English market where it was chiefly rectified into gin.

Government preferred the big distillers: they were an easily controlled source of revenue. The illicit distillers preferred their independence, and retreated into glens where were the best water and peat for their purpose. They were really, in their defiance of the excise, the true founders of the supremacy of Scotch: they found the best sites for distilling malt whisky and even today famous malt-whisky distilleries, in the Highlands and Islands particularly, are located on or near to these ancient smugglers' stills. And the quality of the malt whiskies in Scotland is the corner-stone of Scotch's worldwide success today.

Before leaving these romantic years, we must just glance at what three eminent writers of the later half of the eighteenth century had to say about this drink of the people, made by the people.

First, from Smollett's *Humphrey Clinker*, written in 1770:

Yesterday we were invited to the funeral of an old lady, the grandmother of a gentleman in this neighbourhood and found ourselves in the midst of fifty people, who were regaled with a sumptuous feast ... the guests did such honour to the entertainment, that many of them could not stand when we were reminded of the business on which we had met ...

Then we returned to the castle, resumed the bottle and by

midnight there was not a sober person in the family, the females excepted. The squire and I were, with some difficulty, permitted to retire with the landlord in the evening; but our entertainer was a little chagrined at our retreat; and aferwards seemed to think it a disparagement to his family, that not above an hundred gallons of whisky had been drunk upon such a solemn occasion.

And again, from the same book:

When the Lowlanders want to drink a cheer-upping cup, they go to the public-house...and call for a chopin of two-penny, which is a thin yeast beverage, made of malt, not quite so strong as the table-beer of England...

The Highlanders, on the contrary, despise this liquor, and regale themselves with whisky, a malt spirit, as strong as Geneva, which they swallow in great quantities, without any signs of inebriation: they are used to it from the cradle, and find it an excellent preservative against the winter cold, which must be extreme on these mountains. I am told that it is given with great success to infants, as a cordial, in the confluent smallpox, when the eruption seems to flag, and the symptoms grow unfavourable.

In the autumn of 1773 Johnson and Boswell made their celebrated tour of Scotland and the Hebrides. Leaving Inverness they encountered by Loch Ness their 'first Highland hut', occupied by an old mother. 'With the true pastoral hospitality,' wrote Johnson, 'she asked us to sit down and drink whisky. She is religious, and though the kirk is four miles off, probably eight English miles, she goes thither every Sunday.' As Boswell records it, 'She brought out her whisky bottle. I tasted it; as did Joseph and our guides: so I gave her sixpence more. She sent us away with many prayers in Erse.'

After leaving Fort Augustus, the travellers passed a party of soldiers making roads and, says Boswell, 'We gave them two shillings to drink. They came to this house [in Glenmoriston] and made merry in the barn. We went out, Mister Johnson saying, "Come, let's go and give 'em another shilling apiece." We did so ... The poor soldiers got too much liquor. Some of 'em fought and left blood upon the spot, and cursed whisky next morning.'

Johnson's account runs:

In the evening the soldiers, who we had passed on the road, came to spend at the inn the little money we had given them. They had the true military impatience of coin in their pockets and had marched at least six miles to find the first place where liquor might be bought...

All that we gave them was not much, but it detained them in the barn, either merry or quarrelling, the whole night, and in the morning they went back to their work, with great indignation at the bad qualities of whisky.

On Skye, Johnson noted that:

A man of the Hebrides... as soon as he appears in the morning swallows a glass of whisky; yet they are not a drunken race... but no man is so abstemious as to refuse the morning dram, which they call a *skalk*.

The word *whisky* signifies water, and is applied by way of eminence to *strong water*, or distilled liquor. The spirit drunk in the North is drawn from barley. I never tasted it, except once at the inn in Inverary, when I thought it preferable to any English malt brandy. It was strong, but not pungent, and was free from the empyreumatick taste or smell... Not long after the dram, may be expected the breakfast...

Their peregrinations brought them to the Isle of Coll, where, said Johnson: 'The *malt-tax* for *Col* is twenty-shillings. Whisky is very plentiful: there are several stills in the Island, and more is made than the inhabitants consume.' Already, then, whisky was being exported!

And so to the 'most excellent inn' at Inveraray, where, according to Boswell:

We supped well; and after supper, Dr Johnson, whom I had not seen taste any fermented liquor during all our travels, called for a gill of whisky. 'Come (said he), let me know what it is that makes a Scotchman happy!' He drank it all but a drop, which I begged leave to pour into my glass, that I might say we had drunk whisky together...

It may have been with that Inveraray dram in mind that Johnson wrote to Boswell in May 1775: 'Tell them, as you see them, how well I speak of Scotch politeness, and Scotch hospitality, and Scotch beauty, and of everything Scotch but Scotch oat-cakes and Scotch prejudices.'

A curious aftermath arose on the occasion when a Cornishman was praising a Cornish drink of gin and treacle. Boswell thought it 'a very good liquor' and saw it as a counter-part of *'Athol porridge* in the Highlands of Scotland, which is a mixture of whisky and honey. Johnson said "that it must be a better liquor than the Cornish, for both its component parts are better".'

The Golden Age of Edinburgh was dawning. The poets, first Fergusson and then Burns, took up the whisky theme, and a few quotations from each must suffice at this stage.

First, from Fergusson's *The Daft Days*:

> And thou, great god of aqua vitae!
> Wha sways the empire of this city—
> When fou we're sometimes capernoity—
> Be thou prepar'd
> To hedge us frae that black banditti,
> The City Guard.
>
> O Muse! be kind, and dinna fash us
> To flee awa beyont Parnassus,
> Nor seek for Helicon to wash us,
> That heath'nish spring!
> Wi' Highland whisky scour our hawses,
> And gar us sing.

Robbie Burns is not only the greatest popular poet of Scotland but also, and not unnaturally, of Scotch. A few fragments must suffice, as, for instance, from his *Scotch Drink*:

> Thee curst horse-leeches o' th' Excise,
> Wha mak the whisky stells their prize!
> Haud up thy han', Deil! ance, twice, thrice
> There, seize the blinkers!
> An' bake them up in brunstane pies
> For poor damn'd drinkers.

45

Or from *The Author's Earnest Cry and Prayer*:

> Tell them wha hae the chief direction,
> Scotland an' me's in great affliction,
> E'er sin they laid that curst restriction
>   On aqua-vitae;
> An' rouse them up to strong conviction,
>   An' move their pity.

> Let half-starv'd slaves in warmer skies
> See future wines, rich clust'r'ing, rise;
> Their lot auld Scotland ne'er envies,
>   But blythe and frisky,
> She eyes her free-born, martial boys,
>   Tak aff their whisky.

> Scotland, my auld, respected mither!
> Tho' whiles ye moistify your leather,
> Til whare ye sit, on craps o' heather,
>   Ye tine your dam;
> Freedom and whisky gang thegither! —
>   Tak aff your dram!

We close with these stanzas from his *Third Epistle to John Lapraik*:

> But let the kirk-folk ring their bells,
> Let's sing about our noble sels;
> We'll cry nae jads frae heathen hills
>   To help, or roose us,
> But browster wives an' whiskey stills,
>   They are the Muses.

> Then Muse-inspirin' aqua-vitae
> Shall make us baith sae blythe an' witty,
> Till ye forget ye're auld an' gatty,
>   An' he as canty
> As ye were nine year less thretty,
>   Sweet ane an' twenty!

✹ 3 ✹

Malt Whisky Then and Now

The northern nations are more addicted to the use of strong
liquors than the southern, in order to supply by art the want
of that genial warmth of blood which the sun produces.
James Boswell

That strong liquor produced by the northern Scottish nation
was its own water of life: malt whisky, the very Spirit of
Scotland. And as Edinburgh approached its Golden Age,
so, too, did Scotland's malt whisky. Alas, everything golden,
profitable, attracts the taxman. It was just that fate which
overtook malt whisky as Edinburgh entered into its Golden
Age—and the taxman's intervention took almost forty years
to unravel.

In 1708, just after the union, and, significantly, the earliest
date of any regular account of whisky-production in Scotland,
the whole known output of malt whisky was 50,844 gallons.
In 1756 production had mounted almost ten-fold, to 433,811
gallons. About twenty years later, some Lowland distillers
began exporting their spirit to England, and before long
began the tax problem.

The smaller, almost domestic malt-whisky distillers practically escaped any tax payment on their products for most of
the century, and certainly those illicit, or smuggling, distillers
did. But in the Lowlands was growing up a breed of large-
scale distillers bent on what were then thought massive out-

47

puts by advanced production techniques. Most malt distillers worked with stills ranging from ten to eighty gallons in size. Some of the Lowlanders used larger stills, merging into the thousands of gallons.

Pitt the Younger was the arch-villain in the piece. The Lowland distillers, working on a large scale, were the first victims: in 1784 the English system was introduced, by which the Lowlands distiller had to pay fivepence a gallon duty on his wash, the raw material liquid similar to ale which was distilled to become whisky. From every 100 gallons of wash he was expected to make 20 gallons of spirit at 1-10 over hydrometer proof. Any more spirit than that was forfeit. But the trouble was that English wash was of a much higher gravity, gave a cruder spirit than in Scotland, and had to be rectified into gin in England. In Scotland, the spirit needed no further treatment and the wash, being weaker, gave less spirit per 100 gallons.

It was a double punishment of the Scots by the English politicians and taxation experts. This unjust method of charging tax on the wash lasted only two years, and in 1786 was introduced the Licensing System, the most foolish, unpractical and misconceived taxation process of the century. Once more the distinction was made between Highlands and Lowlands, and the essence of the system to begin with was that in the Lowlands each still should be charged at the rate of 30s per gallon of its content, while in the Highlands the charge would be 20s per gallon of content.

The obvious imbecility of the system is best expounded in the laudatory words of a Select Committee of the House of Commons investigating it in 1798:

> The art of distillation was supposed to be so fully known that persons skilled in it could compute, with sufficient exactness, the quantity of spirits which a still could produce in a year, in proportion to its solid or cubic capacity. This computation being made and the amount of duty meant to be charged on each gallon of spirit settled, the whole sum a still ought to yield per

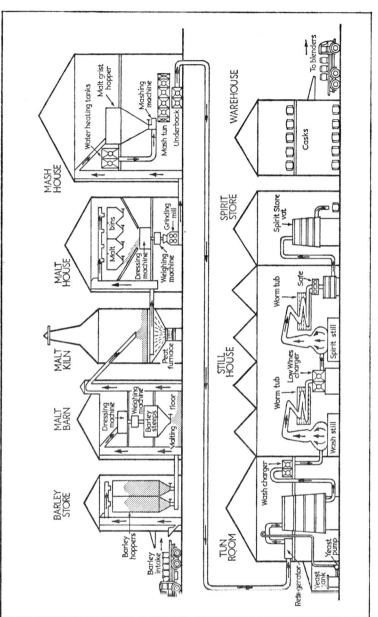

Diagram of the distillation processes

annum was easily calculated at so much per gallon of its capacity.

This annual amount was to be imposed and collected under an annual licence granted to the distiller. By this means, an ascertained revenue would be secured to the public and the manufacturer delivered from the interruptions and inconvenient interference and inspection of the Excise Officer.

It sounds grand, doesn't it? Just too good to be true. It was just that. It had been introduced experimentally into the Highlands when the Lowlands were put under the Wash Act of 1784. Now it was to be applied to both sections of the land. It was naïvely thought, all men being honest, that it would reduce the incentive to illicit distillation in remote parts; that as the Highland barley was of inferior quality and the harvests there more precarious, and that as the Highland distiller was 'usually much inferior to the Lowland distiller in skill and capital', the Highland rate should be only two-thirds the Lowland rate. But as a *quid pro quo* quite unnecessary restrictions were placed on the size of the Highland stills, on the quantity of malt used and even on the spirits produced.

Now many of the lesser malt distillers worked very slowly. Their stills were small, and it might take upwards of a week to complete the distillation. The bigger Lowland distillers worked faster, and in setting up the Licensing System it was calculated that a still could not be worked off in less than twenty-four hours! The distiller was paying his tax per gallon content of the still, and he immediately set to work to make that still produce more whisky than officialdom had calculated. In short, the distiller began to work against time. The duty depended on the content of the still—not on its output in a given time—so the greater the production of whisky the less the rate of duty/tax per gallon made.

It had this important and very real effect on malt-whisky production. Where the still had been high and narrow with a rather short, squat head to it, it was now expanded in diameter and made shallow and broad to expose the heat of the fire

50

Page 51 *(above)* Delivering barley to a remote Highland malt whisky pot still distillery about 1870; *(below)* a group photograph at Cardow Distillery, Knockando, Morayshire, in 1902. Centre, Jimmy Gordon, the brewer, whose small son Joe, killed in the Great War, sits at his feet. HM Customs & Excise Officer, wearing a hard hat, stands third from left in the back row

Page 52 (above) A typical malt whisky distillery lying in a valley shel-
tered by hillside; (below) a malt whisky distillery on Islay, off the west
coast of Scotland. This tiny island, with a population of under 4,000
and an area no more than 235 square miles, has no fewer than eight
such distilleries

more rapidly to the wash to be distilled, while the head and neck were lengthened to avoid the wash boiling over in a rapid distillation and as a means of effecting some sort of rectifying action on the spirit vapours coming over. In brief, there was a revolution in the shape of the still, and the shape resulting from the Licensing System has persisted, in outline, to today, though much of the haste has departed.

Of course, as the shape of the still changed, so to some measure did the character of the whisky coming over: in general for the better. In this race between the distillers and excise, the competition was intense. At first, the stills were refilled five to six times a day. Then it was stepped up to twenty times a day. In 1797 cases were recorded where the still could be refilled 72 times in every 24 hours! And one Scottish distiller, by name of Miller, claimed to have a still which could be worked off and refilled 480 times every 24 hours! Of course, the wear and tear on the stills was terrific, almost uneconomic. But the Revenue was forever catching up on the distillers and increasing the gallon charge.

In 1788 that 30s per gallon content charge was doubled to £3; in 1793 it was trebled to £9 and two years later doubled again to £18. In 1795 and 1796 distillation of spirits from grain was prohibited because of wartime scarcity, as again later in 1805, but in 1797 the race was resumed and the charge was trebled to £54 per gallon of the still's content!

In both 1798 and 1799 the select committee sat and it was then calculated that a still could be worked off and re-charged every eight minutes in the distilling season. The committee reported that:

> Among the principal merits ascribed to the system of licence are first, the secure receipt of the whole licence duty without risk and almost without expense: second, a free and comfortable exercise of his calling by the distiller redounding in its consequences to the popularity of Government and thereby in no small degree to the advantage of the public: third, the alleged dimunition (certainly but ill made out in proof or argument)

D

of the temptation to and loss by smuggling: fourth, the spur it affords to industry and invention in the progressive improvement of an useful art not otherwise to have been attained or expected: fifth, its tendency to increase the total amount of the article manufactured and consequently (when the fact of such increase should come to be ascertained and the amount of the annual licence duty thereupon augmented) to produce, independent of the cheapness of collection a greater receipt at the Exchequer than could have been raised under a similar rate of duty by survey.

That is, by always having an excise officer, or gauger, about watching and measuring. All the Licensing System needed was the occasional visit to ensure that no additional or larger stills had been installed.

That 1799 committee decided that the duty per gallon of still content must be doubled again, in 1800, to £108! In 1803 it was raised again, though less proportionately, to £162. And

A WHISKEY STILL (1827).

as the effective price of the Scotch spirit went down, the government, to protect the London distillers, increased the import duty on spirits from Scotland entering England. There are always ways around everything, and probably more whisky arrived in England than ever paid duty.

Meanwhile, regulations had been getting more and more complicated and involved. The charge per gallon of the still's content in the Highlands had been raised to £6 10s and in 1797 an Intermediate district was created between the Highlands and Lowlands with yet another rate of duty.

But the whole system had this fundamental effect: in the Lowlands only the wealthier could take full advantage of it, and thus it gave a virtual monopoly of the licensed distillery trade there to large-scale operators. And as the system had made it impossible for the small distiller to work as a licensed distiller he did the sensible thing and worked as an unlicensed distiller. Illicit distilling, in fact, grew to such an extent as to be almost general practice. It was the fine hey-day of Scotch law-breaking, of smuggling, a festival of illicit distilling needed again today to reduce the iniquitous tax on Scotch in its homeland.

Unable to cope with the speed of the wealthy distillers, the government had to graft on an element of the Survey System, by which gaugers and other officers surveyed distillery operations, after the committee reports of 1798 and 1799. The licence duty on the still remained; there was also a duty on the spirit produced; the licence duty was held to the duty on a certain specified quantity made in the still; production above that meant further duty. It was a fumbling attempt to license on output, to tax on whisky made. In 1800 came more changes: the Intermediate district was restored to the Lowland district; the Scottish spirit duties were repealed—but they were, of course, re-enacted under a combined system of Licence and Survey with taxes on both the raw material distilled, the wash, and the end product, the spirits.

55

Then, in 1814, came another act, this time abolishing the Licensing System entirely, restoring the Survey System in its entirety with taxes on both the wash and the spirits; installing a distiller's licence fee of £10, and, most unjust of all, making stills of under 500 gallons' capacity illegal in the Highlands. In 1816 all distinctions between Highlands and Lowlands were abolished by another act. But it was that 1814 prohibition of stills of less than 500 gallons' capacity in the Highlands that rankled. It was, in effect, a measure aimed at destroying Highland malt-whisky distilling. What small farmer-distiller could afford such a big still? How much use could he make of it? It was far too big for his needs. And how could he afford £10 licence tax? That sum, it should be remembered, was probably something like twenty times its paper value today. It led to the high noon of Scotch-smuggling, illicit distilling, in the Highlands and Islands.

To quote Morewood, a near-contemporary and a collector of excise in Ireland: 'The consequence was ruin to many respectable distillers, as well as great injury to the revenue by the production and smuggling of Highland whisky—a liquor, which, from its mildness and good flavour, was more consonant to the tastes and habits of the Scotch people.'

Minor amendments which we may disregard followed, and, continued Morewood, 'It appeared by the returns of the sales of legal spirits, that another and more effectual change was necessary. The trade had, in a great measure, got into the hands of smugglers, and thus reduced to an illicit traffic, flourished in different parts of the country beyond all conception.'

To some of these smugglers' deeds of daring we shall return in later stories about Scotch. But, we repeat, the great boon bestowed by the smugglers was to preserve the best Scottish traditions of malt-whisky distilling in the very best locations, the sites where today are to be found the premier Highland malt-whisky distilleries.

George Smith, a farmer's son turned smuggler distiller in

the glen of the Livet (thus the name of the legal distillery he later founded, The Glenlivet, one of the top three or four Highland malt whisky distilleries still working), summed up the situation shortly afterwards, when respectably legal, to a newspaper:

About this time [1820] the government, giving its mind to internal reforms, began to awaken to the fact that it might be possible to realise a considerable revenue from the whisky duty north of the Grampians. No doubt they were helped to this conviction by the grumbling of the south-country distillers whose profits were destroyed by the number of kegs which used to come streaming down the mountain passes. The Highlanders had become demoralised through long impunity and the authorities thought it would be safer to use policy rather than force.

The question was frequently debated in both Houses of Parliament and strong representations made to north-country proprietors to use their influence in the cause of law and order.

Pressure of this sort was brought to bear very strongly on Alexander, Duke of Gordon, who at length was stirred up to make a reply. The Highlanders, he said, were born distillers; whisky was their beverage from time immemorial, and they would have it and sell it too when tempted by so large a duty.

But, said Duke Alexander, if the legislature would pass an Act affording an opportunity for the manufacture of whisky as good as the smuggled product at a reasonable duty easily payable, he and his brother proprietors of the Highlands would use their best endeavours to put down smuggling and encourage legal distilling.

As the outcome of this pledge a Bill was passed in 1823 to include Scotland, sanctioning the legal distillation of whisky at a duty of 2s 3d per wine gallon of proof spirit with £10 annual licence for any still above 40 gallons; none under that size being allowed ...

A year or two before, the farce of an attempt had been made to inflict a £20 penalty where any quantity of whisky was found manufactured or in process of manufacture. But there was no means of enforcing such a penalty for the smugglers laughed at attempts at seizure; and when the new Act was heard of, both in Glenlivet and in the Highlands of Aberdeenshire, they ridiculed the idea that anyone would be found daring enough to commence legal distilling in their midst.

The proprietors were very anxious to fulfil their pledge to Government and did everything they could to encourage the

57

commencement of legal distilling; but the desperate character of the smugglers and the violence of their threats deterred anyone for some time.

At length in 1824, I, George Smith, who was then a robust young fellow and not given to be easily 'fleggit', determined to chance it. I was already a tenant of the Duke and received every encouragement from his Grace himself and his factor Mr Skinner.

The lookout was an ugly one, though. I was warned by my civil neighbours that they meant to burn the new distillery to the ground, and me in the heart of it. The laird of Aberlour presented me with a pair of hair trigger pistols worth ten guineas, and they were never out of my belt for years. I got together two or three stout fellows for servants, armed them with pistols, and let it be known everywhere that I would fight for my place to the last shot. I had a pretty good character as a man of my word and, through watching by turns every night for years, we contrived to save the distillery from the fate so freely predicted for it.

But I often, both at kirk and market, had rough times of it among the glen people; and if it had not been for the laird of Aberlour's pistols, I don't think I should be telling you this story now.

In 1825 and 1826 three more legal distilleries were commenced in the glen, but the smugglers very soon succeeded in frightening away their occupants, none of whom ventured to hang on a single year in the face of threats uttered so freely against them.

Threats were not the only weapons used. In 1825 a distillery which had just started near the Banks o' Dee at the head of Aberdeenshire was burnt to the ground with all its outbuildings and appliances, and the distiller had a very narrow escape from being roasted in his own kiln. The country was in a desperately lawless state at this time. The riding officers of the revenue were the mere sport of the smugglers, and nothing was more common than for them to be shown a still at work and then coolly defied to make a seizure.

Meanwhile, in the turbulent early decades of the century, science had allied with the tax-collector to introduce to whisky-making, first, the saccharimeter, to measure precisely the gravity of the wash to be distilled, and secondly, Sikes's hydrometer with its precise definition and measurement of the spirit distilled and to be taxed. The saccharimeter was also applied to measuring the gravity of the worts, the liquor to be fermented into wash, with varying categories at one stage for each of four different regions in Scotland. In short, governmental control was tightening over whisky-production and restricting its liberty, heedless of Burns's lines:

Freedom and whisky gang thegither!

And regulation was laid down, consequent upon the saccharimeter and the hydrometer being introduced by which the gauger, or excise officer, had to check both the wash and the spirit, that brewing the wash and distilling the spirit could not be carried on at the same time. In fact, it was only in the early 1950s that these two operations were allowed to take place together.

But to revert for the moment to that rationalising and liberalising Distillery Act of 1823 which remains the basis of Scotch distillery law today. The British government in about 1820 was passing through one of its spasmodic bouts of reform and liberalisation. Thomas (later Lord) Wallace, who was vice-president of the Board of Trade, headed a two-year commission between 1821 and 1823 investigating the whole question and learning from past errors. 'Prosperity Robinson'— later the Earl of Ripon—was Chancellor of the Exchequer by the latter date, and he welcomed their findings as adding to the prosperity of his official revenue.

As outlined in George Smith's reminiscences, the 1823 Act allowed anyone, after the 'customary' approval, to become a distiller on payment of a fee of £10—a little later made 10 guineas—and payment of duty on the amount of whisky made, at the rate of 2s 3d per Sikes's hydrometer proof gallon. The specific gravity of the worts to be fermented continued to be taken and that of the wash resulting from fermentation, so that a calculation could be made of the amount of spirit to be expected normally; but no taxes were levied on them, only on the spirit, except in possible case of gross deception as revealed by saccharimeter readings. It was, in a sense, a triumph of reason over precedent. In another—and incidental —sense it was short-lived.

For in 1825 the imperial gallon was introduced, and led to the repeal of the former distillery laws. But the principle continued: the measurement of proof strength and the taxation of the whisky was based on that and the new imperial gallon remained, only the size of the gallon changing, so that the tax proof gallon was now, in Scotland, 2s 10d, the same as in Ireland, while the tax in England was 7s the proof gallon. Scotch whisky going to England had, of course, to pay the difference in duty, and it was only after successive increases in the Scottish rate that it became the same as the English, at 8s per proof gallon in 1855.

As George Smith of Glenlivet has described, the legal changes were not accepted at once everywhere in Scotland. In 1830 there were 392 detections of illicit distillation in Scotland; in 1834 a peak of 692, thereafter dwindling to 177 ten years later and to as few as six in 1874.

But the First Report of the Commissioners of Inland Revenue, published in 1857, tells another story, of the unification of the new distilling laws, if not of tax rates: 'The result of the changes was a most surprising increase in legally made spirits. In 1820 the quantity made in the United Kingdom, which was retained for home consumption, was 9,600,000 gallons. In 1826, it was 18,200,000.'

A boom in Scotch malt whisky set in, not always successful, but in 1827 there were made 2.7 million proof gallons of pot-still whisky from malt only and very nearly as much from a mixture of malt and grain. Ten years later, the malt whisky made in pot stills increased to just over 6 million proof gallons and from malt and grain to just over 2 million gallons. Recession set in and pot-still malt whisky only just passed the 5 million gallons mark in 1847, while the malt and grain version was under the half-million mark. The latter, malt and grain pot-still whisky, a Lowland product, we may disregard, and

60

after slumping for various years pot-still all-malt whisky began its real recovery with the Scotch boom of the late nineteenth century, registering over 7 million gallons in 1877 and almost touching the 14 million mark in 1897, when 'everyone wanted to be in whisky'.

But by then Scotch whisky was on its way to its first world boom as partner to patent-still or grain whisky in the form of the blended product. We cannot, however, leave this real heart of the matter, the precious secret of the Spirit of Scotland, without a glance at its present-day production, wherein are combined the traditional craft of the native distillers and the best in modern mechanical aids.

Today, there are some ninety-five Highlands and Islands pot-still malt-whisky distilleries, if we include one under course of construction, and all are much larger and more highly mechanised than those of the depressed days before World War II. In addition there is a round dozen of Lowland malt-whisky pot-still distilleries, eight pot-still plants on the Isle of Islay, and, sad to relate, such is the change in human taste, only two malt-whisky pot-still distilleries at Campbeltown in the Mull of Kintyre: half a century ago they numbered about two dozen! They were the deep bass of the Scotch chorus of malt whiskies, and with the trend to lighter and lighter malt whiskies and whisky blends they have—temporarily only, we hope—passed out of fashion, though still retaining a corner of the market.

Malt whiskies are generally grouped in four categories: Highland malts, north of an imaginary line from Dundee on the east coast, to Greenock in the west, and sometimes further subdivided into Speyside malts, along and around the River Spey, in that north-east shoulder of Scotland bounded by the North Sea and Moray Firth; and the remainder, from the Orkneys to Perth to Skye and Mull. These are the predominant element in malt-whisky production and in number.

Next, the Lowland malt whiskies south of that Dundee–Greenock line; the Islays from the western, Atlantic-girt island of that name, all full-flavoured and richly peaty malts with almost a tang of the sea about them; and finally the Campbeltowns from the burgh of that name, probably the launching point for malt-whisky distillation as brought over by the Scots from Ireland, and for long regarded as the parliament of the Scotch whisky world. Alas, how have the mighty fallen!

Such is their usual geographical diversity and classification. In every case, the ancient traditions have been preserved, and the only concessions to modernity are in the adoption of such things as mechanical handling, the use, for example, of electricity, of oil—in some, not all—instances, for heating, of automatic conveyors, stokers, etc. Human craft is paramount but, where physical labour can be reduced, it is.

In brief, malt whisky as made in the pot stills of Scotland is still today the original uisge beatha, made only from malted barley of the very best variety—starchy and not over-loaded with nitrogen—which has been dried after malting over slow-burning fires of peat and a little coke. The malt is ground, mashed in hot water to make a sugary liquid which is then fermented with yeast to produce a weak beer-like liquid. This liquid is then distilled twice in onion-shaped copper pot stills: first, to separate the alcohol in the liquid, then, a second time, to extract only the best spirit in that weak alcohol, the middle cut of the distillation which is then set aside in oak casks to mature, to grow up to become malt whisky.

So much for the broad outline. Now for some details. The barley is often taken in at the distillery, screened to remove dirt and other unwanted materials collected in harvesting, and then stored in large airy lofts to 'rest'. That rest is essential; it is all part of the mystery of Scotch. It has been proved that barley cannot be rushed—if it is, it will not give of its best.

As needed, the rested barley is taken by such 'modern'

innovations—distilling is the union of ancient and modern, of the ancient craft and modern aids—as automatic conveyors to large steeps, or tanks, where it is left for days to soak—on and off—in some of the pure Scottish water from the distiller's burn or spring. Well soaked in water, the wet barley is spread out as a couch on a stone or cement floor to begin malting, that is, to begin germinating. Spread rather thick to begin with, it is constantly turned by maltmen with wooden shovels to prevent the tiny rootlets of the barley from becoming entangled, and to allow the clear Scottish air unhindered access to every grain. By degrees the thickness of the couch is thinned out; the rootlets grow at one end of the grain, and a tiny shoot, or acrospire, develops along its side. When it has reached two-thirds of the length of the grain, the maltster knows it is time to stop the growth, the malting.

It sounds simple; actually it covers a series of profound chemical changes within the barley: enzymes are developing in it which change the starch in the barley into a saccharine substance. Starch will never ferment; sugary replacements will. To call a halt to this controlled germination on the malting floor, the old countryside fuel of Scotland, peat, is used, just as it has been since whisky was first made. The green, or sprouting, malt is automatically conveyed to a kiln where it is dried, and any further growth is stopped.

The kiln is a stone building with a pointed roof shaped like a pagoda. On the ground level smoulders a mixture of peat and coke; 30 or 40ft above lies the green malt on a perforated floor where it is regularly turned, sometimes by hand, sometimes automatically. The heat from the furnace dries the malt and halts any further growth, while as the smoke from the peat works its way through the drying malt it imparts to it that inimitable reek which gives the true Scottish bouquet and flavour to Scotch malt whisky.

Sometimes today, to save valuable space at pot-still distilleries—which are usually very cramped for space in any case

—the malting takes place away from the distillery, and the malt is delivered to it ready-made. Sometimes, the malting is not done on floors, but in slowly rotating drums in which the wet barley is turned constantly as by the maltmen on the floors. Sometimes it is done in large concrete or metal troughs, or 'boxes', where the sprouting barley is mechanically turned over and over very slowly for days.

In both these methods the principle is the same as on the floor: enzymes develop within the barley to change its starch into fermentable sugary matter. In these cases, too, the green malt is dried with a fire made of peat and coke. The peat is essential; it is the heart of the Scottish mystery.

After drying, the malt is freed of its rootlets and tiny shoots, or culms, and stored in large airy barns to rest: like the barley before it, malt cannot be hurried. It will only give of its best if allowed to recuperate after the ordeals of fire and water through which it has passed. A further ordeal awaits the malt: it is crushed by automatic rollers, crushed not into a fine powder, but, rather, fragmented, in preparation for its next ordeal—by hot water.

This is a most important encounter with that unique Scottish water belonging to every distillery which is, literally, its own life. Crushed, fragmented, the carefully weighed malt is mixed with water of a fixed high temperature and the mixture is discharged into a large metal tun—the mash tun—complete with automatically revolving rakes which not only rotate around the tun but, by means of side-arms, also stir the mixture from top to bottom. This double stirring action is essential: the hot water stimulates the enzymes to complete their conversion of starch to sugar and then dissolves the saccharine matter.

The liquid resulting is called worts and after hours of mashing is drained through the false bottom of the mash tun, and a hotter charge of water is fed in to replace it. The mashing is repeated; again the tun is drained, and like the previous worts, the liquid is at once cooled and pumped to be fermented in the wash backs, or fermenting tuns.

Two more charges of water are made into the mash tun of ever hotter water, so that the fourth and final charge is nearly boiling. These two mashings do not result in worts, but the liquids, with just traces of the malt, are set aside in tanks to be the first two waters of the next mash. Nothing is ever wasted at a Scotch distillery, and the husks of the malt, called draff, left on the false or perforated bottom of the mash tun, are automatically removed—it used to be by hand—and sold as a valuable cattle food.

Well cooled and in the wash back, or fermenting vessel, the worts from the mash tun have specially selected yeasts added to them, and fermentation begins, as the yeast literally tears the worts apart. Sometimes these fermenters are made of wood, sometimes of steel. Opinion varies: it depends on the distiller's own preference. These vessels can take thousands of gallons of worts and yeast, but are never filled: if they were, they would overflow during the violent action of the yeast. Instead they are only partly filled and each has an automatic switcher which flicks back the rising, bubbling worts as they ferment, and beats back the head of the liquid.

While the yeast is tearing apart the worts in the wash back it is doing two things: converting the saccharine matter in the worts into a weak, beer-like alcohol, and throwing off carbon dioxide. The fermenting rooms are always well ventilated; the windows kept open to allow the escape of carbon dioxide and the inflow of pure Scottish air.

Fermentation usually lasts between two and a half to maybe three days—so much in Scotch distilling depends on imponderables to do with weather and water—and as the fermenting action dies down, its task completed, the liquid in the back is now called wash. Wrapped in a host of intangible ingredients and a vast envelope of water is the Spirit of Scotland. It is the distiller's task to set free, to isolate, to set apart, to liberate, that spirit. This again demands another ordeal, an ordeal by fire again.

So, from its wash back the new wash is pumped to its wash charger—the vessel which charges the still. This is the heart of the mystery: the magic freeing of the Spirit of Scotland. The stills themselves are always of copper—anything like iron would ruin the spirit—and are shaped like large onions with elongated heads.

Originally, and even now at many pot-still distilleries, the heat needed to perform the distillation was provided by means of a coal fire beneath the still itself. Sometimes the heating took the form of oil-burners, but today distillation is increasingly being effected by means of steam, generally applied by the use of steam pipes coiled within the still itself, sometimes by means of an enclosed steam jacket around the body of the still. And where for long the wash entered the first, or wash still, cold, direct from the charger, today it is more often preheated by means of a discharge from the still or hot water from condensers so that it is quickly brought to the temperature level where distillation of the alcohol in the wash begins.

The principle is simple: alcohol and water boil at different temperatures, alcohol boiling and evaporating at the lower temperature. So the temperature of the wash is gradually raised and the alcohol in it begins to come off as vapour, with, of course, a little water. This continues until there is no alcohol left in the wash still but only what is called pot ale. Containing valuable nutrient ingredients, this pot ale is often dried and concentrated to yield animal feeding stuff. As the vapours come over from the still they are quickly cooled by means of running water, either in a tank enclosing the pipe, or worm, in which are the vapours to be cooled, or more often today in specially constructed columnar condensers.

But this first rough separation of the alcohol in the wash from its watery envelope is not good enough for the Scotch distiller. He watches its arrival closely in a special receiver and calls it low wines, harking back to the old days when wines were half-way to spirits. The low wines are then pumped to a slightly smaller copper pot still, called, variously, the low wines still after the product it receives and distills, or spirit still after the product it yields.

This is a much slower more careful distillation process. On the skill and judgement of the distiller depends the quality of the whisky he will make. The same process of distillation is set in motion, and as the condensed vapour flows through the glass-and-brass spirit safe on its way to a receiver he tests it carefully, sending the first runnings, or foreshots, to one receiver as unworthy to become whisky.

Finally he judges that the spirit he has set his heart on is coming over, and this, called affectionately the middle cut, is diverted to another receiver, the spirit receiver. But his vigilance continues: at last he perceives that the distillate is not the quality he wants, the middle cut is ending, and the last runnings, or feints, are then diverted to join the foreshots in their receiver. That is, the first and last runnings of the still are rejected as unworthy of the title and tradition of Scotch, and are added to the next charge of low wines to be distilled, to ensure that there is no real loss of good spirit.

This middle cut, or whisky to be, usually comes from the still at an average strength of 125 degrees Sikes, the British scale of spirit-strength measurement, or about 71 Gay Lussac. It is then reduced in strength to what the age-old Scottish experience has found best at which to begin maturation of pot-still malt whisky, 111 degrees Sikes, or about 63 Gay Lussac; and, most important, it is reduced with the same water as has been used in the steeping and the mashing.

The Spirit of Scotland has now been embodied in clear, colourless form. But it is like the lad who needs to grow up; it is raw, rough, fiery, lacking the polish of age and maturity. Once more it must undergo yet another ordeal: an ordeal of long imprisonment.

67

This imprisonment takes place, first, in oak casks, sometimes casks that have held sherry; often, and from preference, in casks that have been well matured and seasoned by holding whisky prisoner for years previously; sometimes in casks remade from American white oak. The casks, being porous, allow further changes to develop in the whisky as the air penetrates the cask and bears away what the distiller considers undesirable elements in his whisky. Called maturation, it is a series of profound chemical changes in the whisky in the casks and can only take place within them; once in bottle, no further change is possible.

Stored in well ventilated bonded warehouses—to which the excise officer and the distillery manager both have keys—scattered across the countryside of Scotland, purified by the Scottish air, the raw young whisky progresses over the years to become full-bodied and rounded. It reaches maturity, attains perfection.

The Scotch malt distiller does not, cannot, work alone. In addition to his assistants, such as maltmen, brewers, stillmen, coopers attending to casks, and so on, there is always at his side, peering over his shoulder, keeping keys to the distillery apparatus and bonded warehouses where lies the maturing whisky, a representative, often a group of representatives, of Her Majesty's Government, keeping watch and ward. These government officials, or excise officers, ensure by being there that the government collect any taxes and duties to which the whisky may be liable, though during the manufacture and maturation no tax is paid, and even when the malt whisky leaves the distillery to be bottled or blended or sent abroad it pays no duty in Great Britain unless it is to be offered for public retail sale within the United Kingdom. But, more important than their financial function, the excise officers act, in effect, as government officials, ensuring that the distiller adheres to the best in the creation of Scotch.

The making of malt whisky is a sacred cause in the eyes of

Page 69 (above) As a result of the peat smoke there is always a blue smoky atmosphere in the kiln loft where the malted barley is dried; (below) after the malt has been dried over the peat fire, it is ground and then mashed with hot water in the mash tun to complete the conversion of its starch into saccharine material and its solution into the water to make worts

Page 70 (*left*) A wash-back, or fermenting vessel, being cleansed and scrubbed with a traditional heather besom at Talisker Distillery, Isle of Skye; (*below*) cask-making at a cooperage

every distiller in Scotland, in the eyes of every distillery worker, but Her Majesty's official representatives put upon those honest, inherited traditions the stamp and seal of governmental approval and assent.

We close with a few stanzas from Burns's *John Barleycorn*:

> John Barleycorn was a hero bold,
> Of noble enterprise;
> For if you do but taste his blood,
> 'Twill make your courage rise.
>
> 'Twill make a man forget his woe;
> 'Twill heighten all his joy:
> 'Twill make the widow's heart to sing,
> Tho' the tear were in her eye.
>
> Then let us toast John Barleycorn,
> Each man a glass in hand;
> And may his great prosperity
> Ne'er fail in old Scotland!

E

❀ 4 ❀

Scotch and World War II

For Scotch whisky World War II, with its inevitable aftermath of desolation, lasted twenty years. It was only in 1959 that world distribution regained its unshackled freedom and relief from rationing, quotas, and restrictions, although necessarily, because of the prolonged maturing periods involved, de luxe Scotches with such impressive ages as twelve years in the wood were still, even then, in that not-so-romantic wartime and postwar phrase, 'in short supply'.

Those distressing years of worldwide destruction and the ensuing years of world famine are almost impossible for the younger generation of today to imagine, and many who could recall them prefer not to do so. But recall them we must as a vital part of the saga of Scotch, of its triumphant conquest of wartime and postwar difficulties, in which Scotch whisky production and distribution became ultimately a part of the government machine, when Westminster and Whitehall ruled the destinies of the free spirit of a freedom-loving people. Burns was not exaggerating when he wrote that 'Freedom and whisky gang thegither'. World War II saw the death of that Scotch freedom, but it has since emerged again.

If ever there was a case for withdrawal of government intervention in industry and commerce, and for the restriction of its activities to the strictly delimited business of government, the Scotch whisky industry best and most clearly states that case, best illustrates and exemplifies the advantages to be gained from the destruction of that totalitarian invasion of personal rights.

On the very fundamental level of production of new Scotch, savagely, repressively dominated by government order, the result was that the amount of Scotch made in the six years of war, some 32.5 million proof gallons, was about equal to that of one pre-war year. In the Scotch whisky seasons—and traditionally the distilling season begins on 1 October, after the harvest is in—from 1938-9 to 1949-50 inclusive the total amount of Scotch made was less than that of five 'normal' years. To this restriction of production must be added, to understand the long postwar shortages, the essential time-lag caused by maturing the whisky itself. Even when a measure of freedom was regained in the actual making of whisky, other restrictions and hindrances were imposed, such as, for instance, on the building of new warehouses to mature an increased production, on the reconstruction of old distilleries, the creation of new ones to improve still further that base output of Scotch in an ever-expanding market. Yet despite the obstacles of enemy action and government restriction, Scotch won through in its conquest of world markets.

The miracle, and no other word is appropriate to the occasion, is that Scotch became during World War II, and still is, Great Britain's largest visible dollar-earning export. That is *the* marvel of modern industry and business: that a centuries' old native practice begun as a sideline to farming should result in becoming the world's premier international potable spirit, providing, at the same time, a solid and reliable base to the international stability of the pound sterling and British international trade.

To three main causes may be ascribed that ascent to such international supremacy that today many Americans regard and state aloud—that there are two things worth investing in as absolute securities: real estate and Scotch whisky. Those

73

three main causes are: first, the inimitable quality of the beverage itself; secondly, the brilliant business acumen of its producers and marketeers with an unrivalled international outlook; and thirdly, the hard work and expertise of the importers, agents and distributors whom the producers and exporters have chosen around the globe. It is, to say the least, inaccurate to consider that making the best mouse-trap in the world will bring the world to your door; marketing is itself an art, and one which Scotch exporters have cultivated to as fine a pitch as making the quality product they sell.

After which explanatory prologue it is time to return to the beginnings of this World War II phase of the Scotch saga. The late 1920s and early 1930s saw Scotch in the slough of despond, with the world economic depression, American Prohibition and unprecedented unemployment. In 1900 there were over 150 distilleries at work in Scotland; in the 1932-3 Scotch season that number had shrunk to one-tenth, to 15 distilleries, and none of those was working full time. Now, nobody wanted to be 'in whisky'.

Repeal of Prohibition at the end of 1933 helped a little; the gradual stirrings of rearmament began and a few more distilleries began a moderate production. Finally, as war came in sight as inevitable, the shrewd Scots started up their distilleries in earnest, if only to stockpile against the inevitable. Overlapping with the outbreak of war in September 1939, the distilling season in Scotland from October 1938 to September 1939 saw 92 distilleries at work. Between them they made a total that distilling year of 29.2 million original proof gallons of Scotch, that is, the amount of Scotch originally laid down to mature and subject to losses each and every year of maturing. This total comprised 10.7 million proof gallons of Scotch made at the pot-still distilleries using malt only to make the whisky, and 18.5 million gallons of whisky made from malt and other cereals.

Stocks of Scotch maturing in bond were then only given at

the end of the financial year, and as distilling finished earlier then than now, we may say that the industry entered the war with stocks about the level of 31 March 1939, of 144.25 million original proof gallons, a much less quantity if measured in terms of actual gallons. In 1933, the depth of the depression, stocks had only amounted to 125 million gallons, and after a gradual rise had only ascended to 127 million gallons in 1937, and to 134.9 million in 1938. Such was the drain on these stocks, and so restricted was wartime distillation, that at the end of March 1945, on the eve of the cessation of the European conflict, these stocks were down to 84.8 million original proof gallons, possibly only 70 million actual proof gallons. Never before in its recorded history had the industry's stocks been so low. It was only at the end of March 1953 that stocks got back to eve-of-war level when they amounted to 145.5 million original proof gallons.

The wartime vagaries of production and stocks is a matter to which we shall return in detail, but it is necessary first to glance at consumption figures on the eve of war and in the first years of that conflict. It was only as from the eve of war that Scotch whisky was given a separate classification in the official reports of HM Customs and Excise, and these show that in the British financial year ending 31 March 1939, 6.9 million proof gallons of Scotch were taxpaid for consumption in the United Kingdom, and that 7.7 million gallons were exported. That is, 47.2 per cent of the total removed from bond was drunk at home and some 52.8 per cent was exported. In the last financial year of which we have record, that of 1971-2, UK tax payments amounted to 14 per cent of the total of 83,964,000 proof gallons taken out of bond, and exports to 86 per cent, or in terms of gallons, the UK drank 11.9 million gallons, and 72 million were shipped abroad. Such is the changed pattern of Scotch consumption: from being about half and half home-consumed and exported, the proportions are now roughly 15 per cent home and 85 per cent foreign. And this, be it remembered, from an erstwhile by-product of Scottish farming! But for the insatiable rapacity of the British taxman-in-chief and the extravagance of successive British governments that disproportion might not be so great, but the truly impressive element is not so much the diminution of home demand, curtailed as it is by excessive taxation, but the never-ending growth of world demand.

Scotch was an early victim of the war: on 28 September following its outbreak Chancellor of the Exchequer Simon increased the tax on Scotch by 10s (50p) per proof gallon, so lifting it from the pre-war £3 12s 6d to £4 2s 6d, or increasing the duty on a standard bottle from 8s 6d to 9s 8d, so moving up its retail price from 12s 6d to 14s 3d. It was but a gentle breeze ahead of the gales of increased taxation yet to descend upon the Scotch industry and drinker in the UK. Today the tax on a standard bottle of Scotch is £2.20 ($5.30). This current tax compares as above with the tax on a *proof gallon* at the outbreak of war of £3 12s 6d ($8.70).

Another blast was quick to follow. As February 1940 drew to a close Minister of Food Morrison ordered the restriction of whisky output to one-third of the previous year's production. Some confusion arose as to what he meant by the previous year: if that one-third restriction was applied to the year, or season, beginning as traditional on 1 October 1939, some distillers would have already exceeded their quota! The situation was resolved, but The Whisky Association, as it was then (later to become The Scotch Whisky Association), at once imposed rationing on the home market.

That rationing was simply to conserve stocks and to help increase exports (Lend-Lease was not then in operation) and by the association's ruling the percentage of supplies released by members—and some holders of stocks were not members of the association—was to be based on purchases in the year ending 29 February 1940, and was then fixed at 80 per cent. That was what we may now term, with hindsight, a generous

76

percentage: from May 1948 to April 1950 it was as low as 20 per cent.

For already exports of Scotch were soaring, and they too in due course had to be rationed to every world market, save Canada on occasion, in the later years of the war and after it. In 1939, with a European war a near-certainty and a world war a possibility, overseas agents and importers had increased their Scotch orders so that in that calendar year 9,367,000 proof gallons, worth £12,719,000, were exported, of which 4,784,000 gallons, valued at £6,985,000 ($16,764,000), went to the USA.

In 1940 overseas agents and the like made a last desperate throw to get as much Scotch in store as possible, and total exports leapt to 11,258,000 gallons costed at £16,205,000, of which the USA alone accounted for 6,972,000 gallons valued at £10,470,000 ($25,128,000). It was not until 1952 that total exports were again to reach that level, when the 11,531,000 gallons shipped were worth £33,039,000, the US share being 6,301,000 gallons worth £18,481,000.

In his April budget of 1940 Chancellor of the Exchequer Simon returned to the attack on Scotch increasing the tax per proof gallon by 15s to £4 17s 6d, so making the tax in the UK on a standard bottle 11s 5d and its retail price 16s.

Already, then, the Scotch industry was helping win the war on two fronts: by the provision of extra money to the British Treasury by internal taxation, and, more important, by the increased inflow of foreign currency. Justice must, in this latter connection, be done to the American importers: in both 1939 and 1940 members of the National Association of Alcoholic Beverage Importers, Inc, of Washington, DC, took the utmost steps to increase their Scotch imports and in 1940 this reached its peak with their chartering of vessels despite high freight and insurance charges. Whatever the Americans might have to do without, the importers were determined they would not have to go without their Scotch.

77

Moreover, the cut in barley and other grain for making Scotch meant that these home and overseas withdrawals from dwindling stocks were not replaced, and in that opening distilling year of the war, 1939-40, only a total of 13.4 million proof gallons were made, composed of 7.2 million gallons of malt whisky and 6.2 gallons of whisky made of malt and other grains, chiefly maize.

These patent-still distilleries, making whisky from a mixture of malt and grain, ceased to distil after that 1939-40 distilling year until they were allowed a modicum of raw materials in the 1944-5 season—a very bare modicum indeed. For by the time the 1940-41 distilling season was due to open, the war was tearing at the very vitals of Britain; she stood alone against the Axis might, and no shipping or currency was available for the import of maize for these distilleries. Any barley to spare had to be husbanded for other and seemingly more vital purposes.

Exactly how much Scotch was drunk in Britain in that financial year of 1939-40 is just not known: the pace of events after March in the latter year, and for several ensuing, left no time for these near-academic questions to be resolved, but it is established that that financial year saw exports of 10,643,000 proof gallons, as compared with the previous such year's 7.7 million gallons. Financial year exports did not reach that level again until 1951-2 when they totalled 11,203,000 proof gallons.

No tax increases were made on Scotch in the 1941 budget, but on 1 March that year The Whisky Association cut members' releases to the home market to 65 per cent of the 'normal' in a six-month period of 1939, the new percentage lasting only until the end of July. After that month a really savage cut was imposed which brought home in yet another aspect the realities of total war. Beginning on 1 August 1941 and lasting until the end of 1946, releases from bond of brands of Scotch belonging to members of The Scotch Whisky Association, as

78

it was by the latter date, were cut to 50 per cent of the 'normal', the year ending with February 1940.

Meanwhile, Chancellor of the Exchequer Kingsley Wood intervened in his April 1942 budget to add £2 ($4.80) to the tax per proof gallon on Scotch, making it a total of £6 17s 6d ($16.50), or almost double what it had been since April 1920 until the September 1939 increase. This £2 per proof gallon brought the tax on a standard bottle of Scotch in Britain to 16s 1d ($1.90), making the retail price £1 3s, the highest it had even been in British history!

As to production over these tumultuous years, grain whisky made in the patent still had ceased altogether, as we noted above, and in 1941 the Minister of Food once more allowed the malt-whisky pot-still distillers to produce one-third of the whisky they had made in the distilling year before the war. This one-third restriction, enforced by strict governmental supervision and licensing, meant that in the 1940-41 and 1941-2 distilling years distillers made only 3.2 million proof gallons each year, in 1942 being allowed the same amount of barley as in the previous year less 10 per cent, after which they could make whisky from whatever barley they happened to have left over.

If there seems a slight element of confusion in all this, we must remember that the distillers thought and calculated in terms of the traditional distilling year while the Whitehall minister issued his instructions at the end of the calendar year in relation to the ensuing year. We need not here pursue the minutiae of expert statistical differences as to precise quantities of whisky distilled. Suffice it to repeat that in the first distilling year of the war Scotch production amounted to 13.4 million gallons, consisting of 7.2 million gallons of pot-still whisky and 6.2 million of patent-still whisky; that in the second distilling year, Scotch output amounted to only 3.2 million gallons, and that entirely pot still malt whisky, an output which was repeated in the third distilling year of the war, 1941-2. Thereafter, in the summer of 1942, in fact, the fires went out at the distilleries; the kilns no longer smouldered with peat and coke drying the malt; the mash tuns were silent and still; no furnaces roared beneath the pots, and the only life and sounds around these havens of creation in the Scottish countryside were those of the ever-careful checking of maturing whisky in the bonded warehouses and the reluctant and carefully controlled withdrawals, under licence, of mature whisky for the markets of a thirsty world—a world made to forgo its Scotch. After all, it was total war, and Scotch too fell a victim to its totality.

In April 1943 Chancellor of the Exchequer Wood made his last wartime financial assault on Scotch and the British drinker, upping the tax by £1 ($2.40) per proof gallon to £7 17s 6d ($19), making the tax on the standard bottle of Scotch 18s 5d ($2.20), and the retail price per bottle £1 5s 9d ($3.10).

If Scotch was being officially rationed on the home market by members of The Whisky Association, there was a certain amount of whisky held independently of that association, so the official rationing is not truly reflected in official government figures of tax payments of Scotch.

Nevertheless, these governmental tax payments show a decline in the amounts allowed the Scotch-drinker in the British Isles; it was a part, albeit a small part, of the war sacrifices demanded all round. The figure for 1939-40 is unknown, but in 1940-41, as later revealed—it was kept militarily secret during hostilities—it amounted to 6.2 million proof gallons, falling the next year to 5.4 million, and moving up (with the release of non-controlled Scotch) in 1942-3 to 6.1 million gallons; it immediately dropped the next year to 5.8 million, and in the last full year of war, 1944-5, fell to 4.6 million gallons.

Already by the end of 1941 the first signs of a black market in Scotch were appearing within the United Kingdom. In

80

some cases speculators held stocks of Scotch and they, of course, disregarded the instructed and informed directions of The (Scotch) Whisky Association, selling free of price control and restraint to all bidders. In addition, some lesser and more unrestrained off-licensees were selling their rationed quotas of proprietory Scotch brands on the black market at grossly inflated prices.

Exports of Scotch also diminished year by year after that initial flush of the calendar year 1940, falling the following year to 8,484,000 gallons of which the USA took 4,969,000 gallons, and decreasing again in 1942, as the Scots harboured their stocks against the eventualities of war, to 5,541,000 gallons, the USA importing 3,503,000 gallons.

The Lend-Lease Act was also somewhat relieving the strain on British finances by this time, and it is of interest to quote here a statement to the *Journal of Commerce*, New York, early in 1942 by Harcourt Johnstone, parliamentary secretary to the British Department of Overseas Trade, that despite the reliefs of Lend-Lease there was still an urgent need to export. He continued: 'Scotch whisky is among these exports, and stocks of mature Scotch whisky are still available to meet the majority of the many orders which are being transmitted. We appreciate the continued interest and co-operation of the distributors throughout the United States and can assure them that every effort will be continued to maintain supplies.'

But those stocks were shrinking fast. They had stood at 144.25 million original proof gallons in March before the war; a year later, despite withdrawals for home and abroad and because of new whisky additions, they were down to 142.63 million. In March 1941 they had sunk to 129.64 million, and when Harcourt Johnstone was speaking in March 1942 they had reached a new low of 113.98 million original proof gallons.

To resume the details of the export saga, in 1943 they slipped just slightly to 5,215,000 gallons, the USA taking

3,421,000 of them, but in 1944 they sank to 4,435,000 gallons, the American share dwindling to 2,570,000 gallons; while in the last full calendar year of the conflict they edged up to total 4,681,000 gallons, the American allotment slipping back slightly to 2,169,000 gallons.

Another most important event in the history of Scotch also occurred in 1942, shortly after that British assurance to the US about maintaining supplies. On 17 April 1942 The Whisky Association, dating back to 1 January 1917 and called into being by close government co-operation out of the former Wine and Spirits Brands Association, was dissolved at a Glasgow meeting. Previously it had included Irish distillers who had now either gone their separate ways or had disappeared. On 15 May 1942 The Scotch Whisky Association (SWA) was formed in its stead. The chief reason given for the dissolution was the fact that the old association was no longer in accordance with the method of carrying on its affairs, and contained no provision for alteration, though the dissolution itself was in accord with the terms of its constitution. It was officially stated that:

> The objects for which the Association is established are:
> (a) to protect and promote the interests of the Scotch whisky trade generally both at home and abroad and to do all such things and to take all such measures as may be conducive or incidental to the attainment of such objects;
> (b) to protect the interests of owners of proprietary brands of Scotch whisky by taking such steps as the Association may think fit to regulate prices, both wholesale and retail, and to prevent such proprietary brands being sold either whole-sale or retail at prices above those fixed by the Association.

In April 1942, be it remembered, Kingsley Wood had added £2 per proof gallon to the tax on Scotch, so adding 16s 1d to the standard bottle, and in effect producing a retail price of 23s per bottle. As in paragraph (b) of its objects, as stated above, the new association was prompt to act to protect the consumer. The irony is that the association had, basically, its origin in the Wines and Spirits Brands Association formed before World War I to fight cut-prices. The new Scotch Whisky Association had as a prime object the defeat and elimination of profiteering by charging not cut-prices but grossly inflated ones, to act, in short, as a consumer protection movement.

Thus after Kingsley Wood's tax increase, The Scotch Whisky Association immediately issued a list of new *maximum* prices for Scotch: 23s ($2.75) the standard bottle; 12s ($1.70) the half-bottle; 11s 9d ($1.65) the 2½-gill flask. The prices were not dictated by the association; they were only fixed after full and frank discussion with other interested parties such as the National Consultative Council of the Retail Liquor Trade for England, Scotland and Northern Ireland, and the Scottish Licensed Trade Defence Association. Let praise be given where it is due: The SWA was determined to protect the public; to prevent exploitation resulting from shortages; and to safeguard the whole moral health of the Scotch whisky world.

When, twelve months later, Kingsley Wood once more raised the tax on Scotch in his April 1943 budget, The SWA at once issued a new revised official list of maximum prices: 25s 9d ($3.10) for the standard bottle; 13s 6d ($1.60) the half-bottle; the de luxe or better brands being priced 27s 9d ($3.30) and 14s 6d ($1.75) the bottle and half-bottle respectively. Thereafter the tax remained unchanged until the panic budget of November 1947, and the wholesale and retail prices likewise, insofar as The SWA was concerned.

The distilleries of Scotland were then silent and about forty-five of them were used for drying and storing grain, principally oats, since distilling stopped by October 1942 at the latest.

As to the duty increase in Kingsley Wood's 1943 budget, the attitude of the industry as a whole was well summed up by Lord Forteviot, chairman of The Distillers Company Ltd (DCL), in his annual statement the following July:

This latest increase necessitated an adjustment in the price per single bottle, now fixed at 25s 9d for standard brands. While at the present time a bottle of whisky will sell in the home market at this price, taking the longer view, there is no doubt that the position is alarming. If the duty is not substantially lowered when the present national emergency ends, the home trade will be seriously reduced, with a consequential effect on the export trade.

One cannot emphasise too strongly the paramount importance of our export trade to the country in the postwar period. Meanwhile, on the whole, during the past year export trade has been well maintained in the markets still available to us.

A significant auction of stocks of Scotch belonging to a deceased Scotch dealer, which was to lead later to important action both by government and The SWA in defence of fixed maximum prices, took place in Glasgow near the end of the year. The Scotch, consisting of 195 hogsheads, which would have been valued at £3,000 ($7,200) before the war, fetched a total of £110,000 ($264,000) at the auction. Buyers came from all over Britain; the top price fetched was £11 10s ($27.60) per gallon, and the average price was £11 1s ($26.50) a gallon. The buyers were mostly nominees of syndicates who would later re-sell it on the bulk whisky market at, of course, even greater prices. The casks were filled in 1936 and 1937 at 5s (60c) a gallon.

One immediate result was an official reminder that wines and spirits might not be sold by auction except under the Statutory Rules and Orders of 1942, and a Defence Regulation was issued empowering the commissioners of Customs and Excise to refuse the grant of certain excise licences, except under strictly defined circumstances, the aim being to frustrate black-market transactions. The SWA by fixing maximum prices was attempting to protect the public, but auction sales such as that just described were encouraging black-market deals profiteering at public expense by sales above the maximum prices.

The year was now 1944. War still presented a never-ending

aspect of gloom, however much an occasional flash of brilliance lit the scene. A Scotch-thirsty public, inflated by large numbers of Allied Forces, was desperate for its Scotch and many were only too willing to pay the price asked and in return ask no questions. We have seen Lord Forteviot's comment on the tax-inflated price and the public's willingness to pay it; others were as willing to pay an otherwise inflated price, and some traders just as willing to disregard SWA fixed maximum prices.

In these circumstances The SWA Council at the beginning of the year issued a 'recommendation' to members to incorporate a condition of sale governing fixed prices, ending: 'Any person who is found guilty of any offence against the bye-laws renders himself liable to have his name placed upon a Stop List, with the resultant withdrawal of all future supplies of proprietary Scotch whisky by members of the Association.'

A Glasgow sale that February highlights the state of the market and the activity of the black-marketeers: a Highland malt whisky made in 1922 was sold for 214s ($26.70) a gallon; a blend over twenty years old fetched 322s ($38.60) a gallon; brandy sold for 470s ($56.40) and rum for 355s ($42.60) a gallon. One man fainted in the sale room. I quote the first two verses of a six-verse skit on it published by the *Manchester Guardian*:

> Firm and erect the Caledonian stood,
> By Hitler's threats and Goebbels' wiles unhaunted;
> Four years and more of total warfare could
> Not shake his nerve or see his courage daunted.
>
> But, having faced, four-square, the deepening gale,
> With dearth and dire destruction long acquainted,
> Alas! he looked in on a whisky sale;
> And thereupon incontinently fainted.

Shortly afterwards at a Belfast auction London night-club agents' bidding resulted in Scotch selling at £20 10s ($49.20) a gallon or £4 10s a bottle. More than 400 gallons were sold for over £10,000 ($24,000). And, in addition, the purchasers had also to pay the duty of £7 17s 6d ($19) per gallon. The whisky had been blended in 1936 at around 5s to 6s (60c-72c) per gallon.

In addition there was the occasional sale of a company, a sale carried through so that the purchasers could get unrestricted control of the company's stocks. In June so defiant had become the breach of The SWA's fixed prices that the association issued its first Stop List, pointing out that 'in terms of the Bye-laws of the Association, it is an offence for any person whatsoever ... to supply Scotch whisky directly or indirectly to, or to have any trade relations in relation to Scotch whisky with, any person whose name is in the Stop List. The issuing of Stop Lists is in accordance with the objects, regulations and bye-laws of the Association and is designed for the protection of the interests of the members of the Association as owners of Proprietary Brands of Scotch whisky.' To which might have been added that it was designed also for the protection of members of the public. So active was The SWA in this matter of consumer-protection that their issuance of Stop Lists continued well into 1949.

The SWA regarded their responsibilities to the public in the matter so seriously that in the ensuing October the association decided to compete in the auction market of sales of Scotch and outbid whatever price was reached, in order to kill the black-market, and then put the whisky back in the pool for sale at the regular price of 25s 9d a bottle. Members were instructed to keep careful check of all sales by public or private auction and buy openly on the markets and by private treaty in the interests of the legitimate trade and the public. In short, members of The SWA were not wartime profiteers; they were, in fact, wartime protectors of the public—an important fact which it is still necessary to drive home to some members of the public today.

Page 87 (right) Malt whisky is distilled twice in large copper vessels known as pot stills which may be heated either by self-stoking anthracite ovens or by steam; *(below)* the distillation process is controlled from the spirit safe. The traditional skill and experience of the stillman are of paramount importance

Page 88 (above) Blending is the art of combining a very large number of 'single' whiskies from individual distilleries, so that each makes its special contribution to the blend. Samples of single whiskies are constantly tested at blending establishments, always by 'nosing', never by drinking; *(right)* in a modern bottling hall, the whole process from filling to despatching the carton takes place in a single line, each section of the process being supervised by a team of girls

Certainly things were lightening by July 1944, when Lord Forteviot made his annual DCL statement, remarking that 'I cannot too strongly press for permission to start distilling as soon as possible'. His wish was to be fulfilled in some small measure by the end of the year; but in his statement Lord Forteviot reflected the national mood and endeavour of the industry when he said: 'The necessity for conservation of stocks, and the obvious duty to supply, as fully as possible, the Armed Forces, have entailed further rationing of supplies both at home and abroad. The situation at home has been borne by the public with admirable restraint, and our great export markets fully realise that we are supplying them as generously as we can.'

Forteviot's wish to re-start distilling was soon met to some small degree, and early in August the Minister of Food, Colonel Llewellen, announced in Parliament—such was the status now accorded Scotch distilling—that he would allocate 'a portion of grain stocks over the coming twelve months for distillation'. Pressed by a parliamentary question from Bob (now Lord) Boothby, the minister added that the resumption of distillation 'can only be to the limited extent which present supplies allow and after taking into consideration the other calls upon these supplies'.

It was at least a gleam of hope in a dark setting: the patent stills had ceased operating in 1940, and the pot stills their very limited activity in the middle of 1942. But already a tightening of government control over whisky-production was emerging, a control which was shortly to make Scotch distilling a bureaucratic department of Whitehall. For in a speech at Aberdeen in the following September, that is, on the eve of the commencement of the traditional distilling year and at the edge of the Speyside distilling region, Colonel Llewellen said that the recently announced and permitted whisky distilling would not mean more whisky for the home market but would principally benefit exports.

F

This was immediately interpreted by a prominent distillery official, who had had close access to the minister, in these words: 'The Minister's latest statement simply follows the trend of those which he had made earlier on the same subject. It was fully realised, before the recent statement, that any steps taken just now for the resumption of whisky-making were more concerned with laying down stocks for the postwar export trade than with increasing supplies in this country. The importance of maintaining the export trade is recognised, and even during the war exports have been continued to a limited extent.'

Such was the fate of this sideline to Scottish farming that it was now regarded at top government level as a priority among British exports to preserve the pound sterling and UK international standing.

On 25 September 1944 Colonel Llewellen as Minister of Food issued a Potable Spirits (Licensing and Control) Order, to replace the 1940 Order, prohibiting the manufacture of spirits from cereals except under licence, and ordering Customs and Excise to supervise the distilleries for the purpose. Excise officials always had, and still do, if only to guarantee the government revenue from the distilleries. But there was more to it than just normal supervision.

His order was to prevent Scotch distilled then and as long as control continued from leaking into 'improper' channels. Not only could the Scotch be distilled only under licence, it could only be sold to recognised pre-war customers of the distillers. Another of the conditions attached to the licence was that the whisky should not be sold at an 'excessive' price. It was stipulated that the distiller should keep records of manufacture and sales in order that the Ministry could check on what became of the whisky. (Records of the respective 'makes' had, of course, long since been compulsorily kept.)

It was hoped that the allocation of barley and other cereals in the distilling year October 1944–September 1945 would be enough for distillers to make about one-fifth of what they made before the war, or something between 5 and 6 million gallons, the annual pre-war production being in the region of 28 million proof gallons.

In the event, with some later additions, that distilling year overlapping the end of the war saw the production of 3.7 million proof gallons at pot-still distilleries using malt only, and 5 million gallons at those using malt and other cereals, so making a total of 8.7 million gallons.

This control order, for such it was, was basically aimed at the war speculators who pushed their way into the trade and helped to rocket prices. Insofar as new makes of Scotch were concerned, it went far to end the practice of a secret commission being paid to those who 'negotiated' sales of Scotch and also helped to stop the activities of those ingenious gentry who are forever with us and are both prone and able to drive the proverbial coach and horses through acts of Parliament. Indeed, the former Food Minister, Lord Woolton, had at one stage threatened—quietly—to impose price control if the Scotch trade did not discipline itself.

The September control order and the remembrance of Woolton's threat were the factors, then, which lay behind the decision of The SWA to compete in the auction market and outbid whatever price was reached. From one essential point of view that decision may now, with hindsight, be seen to have been actuated as a matter of self-defence.

In the event, the distillers only began distilling again early in 1945. The barley and other cereals were duly released, but there was a shortage of labour and of coal, and 34 distilleries finally began work in January 1945, some 17 of them belonging to Scottish Malt Distillers, a subsidiary of The DCL, and 17 being independently owned.

Scotch whisky was made in Scotland, certainly, but Scotch whisky was ruled from Whitehall, and in March 1945 a deputation of three powerful men in the industry humbly waited on Scottish Unionist Members of Parliament begging them to use their influence to obtain more raw materials for distilling and, if humanly possible, a cut in the duty.

It was the following month that Prime Minister Churchill penned his famous Minute: 'On no account reduce the barley for Whisky. This takes years to mature, and is an invaluable export and dollar producer. Having regard to all our other difficulties about exports, it would be most improvident not to preserve this characteristic British element of ascendancy.' That SWA deputation and the Churchill Minute bore some fruit, for some additional barley was released to the distillers and extra amounts of coal were also allowed them. In the event, the Speyside distilleries which had begun on time ceased, as normally, in the summer, but for the first time ever and after making special arrangements distilleries at Oban and other West Highland centres which began late worked through the summer of 1945.

That July, which saw the defeat of the Churchill Government and the accession to power of the Labour Party, lovers of state control in every industry and direction, under Clement Attlee saw also the first postwar annual meeting of The Distillers Company Ltd under the chairmanship of Lord Forteviot. Some of his remarks are worth recording. In the year reviewed, 1944-5, he said, supplies of home-grown cereals equal to about one-third of normal pre-war requirements were released to the industry and during the whole of the war, almost six years, the entire output of Scotch was less than one normal year's output. 'Severe losses' had been caused by enemy action, and many distilleries had been requisitioned for war purposes. Sales, both at home and abroad, had been established on a quota system 'on as generous a scale as circumstances permitted'. 'The establishment first and the gradual building up of the export trade in Scotch whisky throughout the world is one of the great romances of industry. It would be difficult to overestimate the benefits that have accrued to this company from the efforts of those pioneers of the past who left home to find new markets overseas.'

We have already noticed exports during the war and to the end of the calendar year 1945. One-third of a normal year's supplies were allowed for 1944-5 and at the end of March 1945 stocks in bond maturing stood at their lowest ever—84.79 million original proof gallons, a much smaller actual quantity. Now lay ahead the task of rebuilding those stocks until there were sufficient supplies to meet expected world demand. In the event world demand far exceeded what was then calculated at the end of hostilities, and rationing of one kind and another was not to cease until the middle of 1959.

More and easier shipping became available after the end of the war, and in 1946 Scotch exports set out on their long epic saga, surpassing those of the previous calendar year by more than one million gallons to make a total of 5,881,000 gallons, of which 2,848,000 went to the USA. The amount allowed for the home market remained the same, 50 per cent of the pre-war quantity, but some 4.7 million gallons of Scotch were drunk in the UK in 1945-6 as against 4.6 million in the previous year.

The war was by no means over for Scotch. Now began the battle of rebuilding stocks while still keeping customers at home and abroad happy, and while obeying the government dictate. That soon came to the fore. Sir Ben Smith, the Food Minister, said in a broadcast early in 1946 that they 'could not spare a grain' of barley for whisky; it was a question of 'Food before whisky'. Towards the end of that January, Dr Summerskill said in the House of Commons, in reply to a parliamentary question, that the distillers were being 'licensed' to use enough cereals of the 1945 crop to produce three-sevenths (43 per cent) of the pre-war quantity. Speaking on behalf of Smith, she added: 'My right honourable Friend regrets that it is impossible to increase this figure at present in view of the world cereals position and the requirements of Europe. He is, however, fully aware of the importance of whisky exports and the position will be kept under continual review.'

The result was that in the 1945-6 distilling season the pot stills using malt only made some 5.8 million proof gallons of new whisky, and those distilleries using malt and other grains made 8.5 million, a total of 14.3 million proof gallons to be compared with the 1938-9 season of 29.2 million gallons. Then, rather late in the day, the Ministry of Food stepped in making an order, effective 3 June 1946, banning the auctioning of whisky (and gin) in order to help the trade in controlling prices and endorsing the then current retail prices for both spirits as fixed by the appropriate association. Scotch was now moving at the top in every realm of government; indeed, it was shortly to become even more involved with government, and on an international scale, with supplies for production granted on the basis of specified export targets and drastically slashed home-market releases.

Before the summer of 1946 was out, The SWA found it necessary to issue a formal statement denying that home-market distribution was to be cut in order to help exports, affirming that its 'policy is to preserve the same balance as hitherto between home sales and export... For every bottle of whisky exported, a bottle remains behind for home consumption... To maintain exports without a firm home market would hardly be possible ... no intention of placing the home market in jeopardy.' That was just what was to happen.

In October representatives of The SWA met the Minister of Food to discuss allocations of grain for distilling, at which meeting the minister is said to have made it clear that he was alive to the importance in the national interest of an early resumption of distilling and would keep the matter 'under close personal review'. But, he went on, the difficulties of supply and transport of the cereals necessary to maintain essential food requirements of people and livestock in the UK had been 'increasing from week to week'. The then present supply position, he concluded, 'precludes the possibility of any immediate allocation being made for distilling'.

By the end of the year the quota based on pre-war releases to the UK market was cut from the 50 per cent, at which level it had stayed since 1 August 1941, to 45 per cent as from 1 January 1947. And Food Minister Strachey dispensed a miserable 50,000 tons of barley for distilling. On Good Friday evening following Strachey announced that he would allow the Scottish distillers to buy a further 50,000 tons of barley from the 1946 harvest and 75,000 tons from the 1947 harvest —on the assumption that it was a good crop.

This was no free gift. Gone were the days of a bottle for home and a bottle for export. Export targets were now the fashion, and Scotch was set its target. That target could only be met out of depleted stocks, standing at their lowest ever, or only 79.8 million original proof gallons at the end of March 1947, by reducing the home-market ration. So from 1 May 1947 to 30 April 1948 the home ration of Scotch was fixed at 25 per cent of the pre-war level, or half of the December 1946 level!

As Sir (then Mr) Henry J. Ross, deputy chairman of The DCL, said at the annual meeting in October, reviewing the allocations of cereals for distilling, the releases of grain were 'not made by the Government without conditions'. The government would only grant licences to distil (remember Burns: 'Freedom and whisky gang thegither!') on an understanding to increase exports to the 'hard-currency' markets.

The proportion laid down by Strachey from 1 May 1947 was three gallons for export and one gallon for home. The stock position, he explained, was such that it could only be done by cutting releases to the home market, and so shipping more to the 'hard-currency' areas, such as the US.

Calendar year statistics reveal the position most clearly: in 1946, as stated above, 5,881,000 gallons of Scotch were exported, of which 2,848,000 went to the US. In 1947 the total

exported was 6,771,000 gallons, 3,990,000 of them being shipped to the US. The 'hard-currency' area drive was on, and in
the calendar year 1948 shipments to world markets overseas
totalled 7,896,000 gallons, of which the American share was
4,649,000, or almost double what it had been two years earlier
in 1946. In 1949 exports totalled 8,521,000 gallons, the US
share being just over the 5 million gallon mark. In 1950 total
shipments amounted to 9,708,000 gallons, and the US allocation to 5,846,000, or more than double what it had been only
four years before, in 1946.

That DCL meeting was held on 15 October and less than a
month later, on 12 November 1947, the ill-fated Chancellor
of the Exchequer, Hugh Dalton, aimed a body-blow at the
long-suffering and deprived British drinker of Scotch: he
increased the tax on whisky by 33s 4d the proof gallon to make
a total of 190s 10d, forcing the fixed maximum price of Scotch
up by a duty per standard bottle of 22s 3d to sell at £1 11s.

It is no discredit to Dalton to say that he was unsuccessful
as a chancellor, and his budget was freely described then, as
now, as 'paltry'. As he himself said, 'I don't think this will be
a popular Budget.' It was not. There was no need for it. The
Exchequer needed no more money, apart from what was
allowed for in the April budget, and common sense, a rare
quality in politicians of course, said there was no need for an
extra tax on Scotch. By then, of course, October 1946 to
September 1947, the distilling season was over and the result
of Strachey's Food Ministry interference with 'targets' for export, allocations for distilling, and the rest was that production
of Scotch that season was down—down to 3.5 million gallons
of malt whisky made at the pot-still distilleries, and 5.6 million
gallons made at those distilleries using malt and other cereals,
a total of only 9.1 million gallons, compared with the previous
season's 14.3 million.

Worse, however, lay ahead for the home market, for the
Scotch-lover in Britain. The year 1947, despite the extra duty

and the cut to 25 per cent in home-market supplies, had ended on a deceitfully cheerful proclamation in December that the distillers were to receive another allocation of 75,000 tons of barley bringing the year's total allocations to 250,000 tons. This latest allocation—the word itself smacks and smells of the period of rationing—was expected to keep the distilleries going until April 1948. And for full-scale production as at the pre-war level they would only need 300,000 tons to make 30 million gallons.

But on 6 April 1948, Chancellor of the Exchequer (Austerity) Cripps added another £1 to the tax on Scotch bringing it up to the famous triple ten level: £10 10s 10d ($25.30) per proof gallon, where it remained until Chancellor of the Exchequer (Regulator) Selwyn Lloyd on 25 July 1961 increased it by his infamous 10 per cent to 231s 11d ($27.80). But Cripps's 1948 budget increase made the tax per standard bottle of Scotch in Britain 24s 7d ($2.95) and increased the controlled maximum price to £1 13s 4d ($4), at which level it remained until the association itself was permitted to increase the price to £1 15s ($4.20). The budget was alleged by its supporters to be anti-inflationary, anti-spending; but the government, it is not untrue to say, were then themselves the largest and most profligate spenders in the land.

Worse was yet to come. The exorbitant demands of the government in fixing export 'targets' meant that the amount of Scotch permitted by members of The SWA to be released for the home market was cut back to 20 per cent of the pre-war standard level from 1 May, a position at which it remained until the end of April 1950, when it was marginally increased to 25 per cent, that is, still only half of what was allowed at home for most of the war.

A few figures will illustrate the parlous condition of the Scotch-drinker in the UK in these years. In the financial years 1945-6 and 1946-7 just 1.7 million proof gallons of Scotch were taxpaid in the UK each year. In the 1947-8 year that figure

97

had sunk to 3.2 million gallons, and in 1948-9 it touched rock-bottom at 2.5 million gallons, just clambering back to 3 million in 1949-50.

It was typical of the over-governed years of postwar Britain that it was regarded as a concession in July-August 1948 when the Board of Trade closed down the Scotch Whisky Export Group, handing the group's functions over to The Scotch Whisky Association, with whom all agreements regarding the export of Scotch had been made in any case.

It is now a matter of history how The SWA sent circulars to distillers for issue to all their customers before any fillings of new whisky into buyers' casks could be made: that because of the barley agreement with the Ministry of Food preference had to be given, to be promised, in effect—under threat of withdrawal of barley supplies—to 'hard-currency' markets, that 'soft-currency' markets were to be 'soft-pedalled', that the home market was to be cut to two million gallons.

This regulation, this control and direction, was by no means accepted without question everywhere. Some blenders had never catered for the export trade, and a leading blender of this type rose in defence of those holders of stocks of Scotch who had bought them at comparatively high prices, saying: 'It is a pity that Scotch whisky was not controlled by the Government in Autumn 1939 or Spring 1940.' These home-market traders were now, under Ministry of Food regulation of the trade as administered for the ministry by The SWA, in danger of extinction in the pursuit of government doctrinaire policy.

In the first Strachey year, that ending in April 1948, the target had been in the ratio of three gallons, or bottles, for export, to one for the home market. In the event, that year saw Scotch exports of 6,248,000 gallons to 'hard-currency' markets, of 1,481,000 to 'soft-currency' countries, a total of 7,729,000 gallons as against 2,996,000 gallons for the home market: a proportion, that is, of 72.1 per cent for export, and 27.9 per cent for the UK.

But the next Strachey year, beginning 1 May 1948, saw even further curtailment of supplies of Scotch to the home market, and greater pressure on exports. Remember it was the period of Cripps's 'Export or die!' call to the nation. That new year saw home supplies cut to as low as 20 per cent of the standard pre-war year.

The perilous position of the entire industry was best put in perspective by Sir (then Mr) Henry J. Ross, chairman of The DCL, at the company's annual meeting in Edinburgh on 24 September 1948. Reviewing the year, Henry Ross stated that, realising the importance of Scotch in the future as well as the present, the government had authorised 250,000 tons of barley for the period to 30 April 1949, 'subject to certain conditions regarding the further stepping up of exports to hard-currency areas, by reducing the quantity available for the home market'. Where the arrangement had been three gallons for export and one gallon for the home market, said Ross, from 1 May 1948, it had to be reduced to 20 per cent for the UK market, as the ministry insisted on still greater exports to 'hard-currency' regions and stocks were such as to necessitate the cuts at home. (At the end of March that year, Scotch stocks, not all matured by any means, amounted to only 86.7 million original proof gallons, the quantity originally laid down to mature.)

As Ross said on this famous occasion in Edinburgh, on 24 September: 'To all intents and purposes the export trade is under Government direction, and the industry was allotted a target figure to cover shipments to dollar markets, such as Canada, USA, South Americas, etc.' But it all meant, he said, 'a drastic cut of supplies to soft-currency countries as well as to the home trade'.

Scotch had certainly done its part in the British war effort, a part continued into postwar reconstruction. That we must all agree; but as to future prospects at that uncertain time with a disrupted world, half of which was starving. In the autumn of 1948, Henry Ross said with typical Scottish caution

99

that it was 'neither possible nor desirable . . . to forecast very far ahead'. He declined to do so at all.

A wise man who proved the proverbial tower of strength to the industry and The SWA through all these tortuous years, in addition to his hard work for the company he chaired. But in February the following year, 1949, came more cheerful news to lighten his, the industry's and the drinkers' gloom: 250,000 tons had been allocated to the industry for the period to the end of April 1949, and in February came the official decision to allocate 300,000 tons, or, in short, the amount needed to restore the industry's distilling output to its full pre-war strength; but as Ross was to put it the following September at The DCL annual meeting the distillers were 'obliged to pledge ourselves to increase still further our exports of old whisky'. As it turned out, that 20 per cent ration for the home market continued up to the end of April 1950, when it was increased to the magnificent proportion of 25 per cent!

As recorded by Henry Ross, the meeting between The SWA and the Food Ministry in February 1949 saw the delegates submit 'with the utmost emphasis' the needs of the home market. They were submerged by a flood of rhetoric and verbiage about 'hard-currency' export markets and, again, the home trade was restricted to an official two million gallons to the end of April 1950. As he put it in September, it was 'the strangulation of our home-trade interests'. The US and Canada, of course, were 'the most important hard-currency markets', but, said Ross, as the spokesman of the industry, the 'soft-currency' markets must also be considered. 'Continued shortages,' he went on, 'will assuredly open the door to substitutes of one kind or another, of which there are many in various countries of the world.' This was particularly so in the case of the home market, and for economic reasons, some, notably South American republics, 'have been closed to us as markets for our brands of Scotch whisky'. South Africa pre-

100

sented another problem: that government had prohibited many luxury imports, including Scotch, and the only way to maintain the old trade with that valuable market was to leave the whisky earnings there in government or municipal securities or other approved investments.

Such were the struggles endured by the Scotch industry to regain and enlarge its markets in the postwar years. That postwar success was not achieved by accident, and did not just come about of its own accord; it is probably the best instance to date of the dogged, determined organising ability of the Scot in selling his unique spirit world-wide.

In any case 1949 saw something of a return to 'normal' distillation in Scotland and the whole matter was once more put in perspective by Henry Ross at a Glasgow dinner in February 1950, when he remarked:

> The past year has seen a return to full-scale distillation of Scotch whisky. Unfortunately, in our business, distillation and distribution do not go hand in hand... The quota of Scotch whisky available for home trade consumption has fallen to its lowest ebb.
>
> We do not consider that a healthy or progressive export trade can exist permanently unless it is backed by a healthy home trade as well... We wish to see a Government which will permit us to carry on our business on reasonable lines, and, at the same time, cease to treat our products as an apparently inexhaustible source of revenue.

He then made an important point as true today as when he made it:

> Another most unfortunate result of the present high rate of duty is that it is indirectly responsible, in our opinion, for the raising of duties on Scotch whisky in many of our export markets.
>
> When such increases in duty take place in foreign countries, it is our practice to protest through the Board of Trade, but in many cases we find that any arguments put forward to the foreign Government responsible are countered by a reply to the effect that the new rate of duty to be charged is still substantially less than that which is applicable in our own country.

A survey of Scotch distribution in the Stratchey year ending in April 1950, produced at about the same time by Mr L. A.

Elgood, gives the pattern as then agreed between The SWA and the Ministry of Food:

The USA was to get	5,280,000	proof gallons
Canada	1,096,000	,, ,,
Belgium, Belgian Congo and Switzerland	275,000	,, ,,
Total	6,651,000	,, ,,
Other desirable export markets	1,349,000	,, ,,
Soft-currency markets	1,000,000	,, ,,
Total	9,000,000	,, ,,

—leaving 2 million gallons for the home market. But Mr Elgood expected this would rise to about 3 million as drawn from deceased estates, brokers, brewers, and occasional holders of Scotch stocks, which would all sell at higher prices than the established maximum price. Such then was the pattern and nature of this erstwhile sideline of farming, of smugglers and illicit distillers! And such was Scotch's international involvement that with British devaluation of the pound sterling in 1949 it was possible to adjust the sterling price of Scotch exports to the US and Canada as well as in other parts of the world and to obtain the same number of dollars as before, without increasing the quantity exported or the price to the consumer.

But with the beginning of the new bureaucratic year on 1 May 1950 the export target was raised to 9.6 million gallons from the previous year's export target of 9 million gallons. The new target was said to be 'based on the practical possibilities of increasing overseas sales, three-quarters of which are reserved for dollar markets'.

At the same time the ministry 'advised' The SWA that, provided exports were not endangered, they had no objection to releases for home consumption being increased! They were then increased to 25 per cent of the base year, where they remained until the end of government-imposed home-market rationing in December 1953. The ministry expected, in fact, that extra home-market supplies from members of The SWA at a controlled price would displace large high-priced sales by non-members, and the result would simply be no actual extra sales at home. The Strachey year now, with the new minister, became the Webb year! Such is fame.

That increase for the home market from 20 per cent to 25 per cent of the base, pre-war year, explained Henry Ross to the annual meeting of The DCL in Edinburgh the following September, meant only an extra 600,000 gallons to the UK market, bringing the official quantity released to 2,600,000 gallons. This he described, along with millions of Scotch-lovers in Great Britain, as meaning 'some degree of relief'. The two million official gallons of the previous year, he admitted, had actually been exceeded by about 50 per cent, drawn from those other sources we have already mentioned, and were sold, he said, 'at prices substantially in excess' of the association's fixed prices. He thus hoped, like the government, that the extra 600,000 gallons would 'have the effect of reducing the demand for these highly priced supplies' and help 'regulate what has been a most unsatisfactory position'.

But the prospect, he thought, of reaching the pre-war position was 'extremely remote': 'It seems quite impossible of attainment so long as the present rate of duty continues.' (Today, the duty, at £2.20 [$5.30] per standard bottle in the UK is almost double.) More accurately and to the point, he made the comment that Scotch 'is now regarded as a luxury instead of being within the reach of everyone as it was in the past'. Another casualty, we may consider, of war: the removal of the working-man's drink into the de luxe category.

When the now usual annual discussions came around between the Ministry of Food and The SWA in the spring of 1951, it was graciously permitted by the bureaucrats that there should not be any cuts imposed on Scotch releases to the home market, that the 2.0 million proof gallons allowed a year to Britons and visitors to HM British Isles might remain unchanged. But it was also ruled that the previous annual rate of exports of 9.6 million proof gallons should be increased by an extra 250,000 gallons.

Some hint that this government control of a free, private industry was to continue into the indefinite future was to be seen in the decision to scrap the new Webb year, beginning on 1 May, and deal in permits and targets per calendar year. So it was decided that for the calendar year 1951 the industry, or, at least, members of The SWA, would export a quantity equal to the target for the first Webb year, or 9.6 million gallons, plus 167,000 gallons. Complex calculations, but it comes to this: that exports were to be increased $1\frac{3}{4}$ per cent, or two-thirds of the Webb year extra 250,000 gallons. 'Freedom and whisky gang thegither,' wrote Burns. He should have been living in the 1950s.

Control of Scotch was so tight and rigorous that this pattern was then fixed: 1. Exports to the USA, Canada and other countries of the American Account Area were still to get top priority, and as far as possible the extra 167,000 gallons were to go to them. 2. Dominions and colonies were now to 'rank second in importance'. 3. No other priority among markets. The American Account Area included not only the USA and Canada but also Alaska, Puerto Rico, Hawaii and the Virgin Islands (as part of the US), Bolivia, Bahamas, Bermuda, Colombia, Costa Rica, Cuba, Dominican Republic, Ecuador, El Salvador, Guatemala, Haiti, Honduras, Mexico, Nicaragua, Panama, Philippines, and Venezuela.

The 'obligations' extracted by the ministry were that each member of The SWA should so arrange his exports for the remainder of 1951 that during that year he would export an amount equal to the first Webb year plus $1\frac{3}{4}$ per cent, and he would export to the American Account Area an amount equal to the Webb year target 'plus as much as possible of his $1\frac{3}{4}$ per cent increase in total exports'. At the same time, members were to restrict home-market releases to what was authorised in the first Webb year; that is, 2.6 million gallons. And over-shadowing the promise or threat distillers were permitted 'open licences' to buy home-grown barley.

It was the high-water mark of state control of the Scotch whisky industry, a control and supervision totally alien to the character of the Scots, their spirit and their genius, and one which we fervently pray will never be repeated.

Let us turn to Henry Ross, chairman of The DCL, at his September 1951 annual meeting when he remarked that sales of Scotch at home and abroad were 'largely patterned to the national interest' and, more ominously, were 'under govern-ment direction'. Thus, he went on, some markets got special attention and a situation was created 'which is not in the long-term interests of either the Company or the Industry'. But this state of affairs, he said, would continue until the stock position of mature Scotch could meet all demands.

Actual supplies made available to the home market had again exceeded the official ration—this time by 46 per cent—and this excess meant exorbitantly high prices to the trade and the public. As to the then excessive duty, its continuance, said Ross, would mean 'the gradual extinction of Scotch whisky as a beverage on the Home Market, but it also serves to encourage Overseas Markets to increase their rates of duty'.

They had made representations to the Chancellor of the Exchequer on the matter, and the only consolation they had out of it all was a quotation Ross then made from the Secre-tary to the Treasury in a House of Commons debate who had said: 'The highest marks of all go to the Whisky Industry and if one measures it in terms of Dollars its record is far more remarkable and better than that of any other industry. It is a remarkable feat by this great Scottish industry to have earned this high amount of dollars and yielded so much Revenue to the Exchequer at the same time.'

By then there had been a change of government in Great Britain, but the same bureaucrats continued in office, and

105

with the same love of power. The position continued un-changed, with annual bargaining between the members of The SWA and government as to exports and home releases; and although distillers had been made free in 1950 to buy barley at home unrestricted, many wished to make such pur-chases again conditional.

The year 1952 saw, however, some notable and important changes. Even under the new Tory Government of Winston Churchill, now back in power, the need to export was para-mount, and Scotch remained Britain's largest single visible trade dollar-earner. But that year it was decided that while the USA and Canada still headed the list of desirable markets, now 'all exports are of value to the British economy'. As a result, some firms that had been devoting their extra consign-ments to those markets decided to give increased attention to others where there was 'a clamorous unsatisfied demand in consequence of the concentration in the dollar countries in the past few years'.

Later that year was passed the Customs and Excise Act con-solidating previous measures. For the first time ever Scotch whisky was defined by statute: 'Spirits described as Scotch Whisky shall not be deemed to correspond to that description unless they have been obtained by distillation in Scotland from a mash of cereal grains saccharified by the diastase of malt and have been matured in warehouse in cask for a period of at least three years.' The important thing here is that 'Scotch' is of geographical, not general or generic, significance. This definition has been used worldwide ever since to defend the consumer, the product and the industry.

The other definition concerns the term 'proof', defined in the act as follows: 'Spirits shall be deemed to be at proof if the volume of the ethyl alcohol contained therein made up to the volume of the spirits with distilled water has a weight equal to that of twelve-thirteenths of a volume of distilled water equal to the volume of the spirits, the volume of each

106

liquid being computed as at fifty-one degrees Fahrenheit.' That is, proof strength spirit is that which at 51°F weighs exactly twelve-thirteenths of an equal measure of distilled water. Scales exist for executives, administrators and operators to calculate the proof gallonage of any volume of spirit at any strength and any temperature.

The definition of Scotch had also this immediate importance: with distilling increasing and becoming more free, a little trade in export of immature Scotch was beginning to grow up, and immediate action, not entirely successful, was taken against it at once. It is a long tedious story, as some countries have no minimum age for their Scotch imports, but The SWA is on constant alert to prevent its masquerading as genuine Scotch. The tangled tale need not delay us here, except to note that the Swedish State Monopoly is the largest importer of immature Scotch, and then fully matures it before selling it to the public.

Incidentally, the Queen's Birthday Honours list that year included a knighthood for Henry Ross, as chairman of The Scotch Whisky Association and in acknowledgement of that association's export achievements and its fine work at home.

Turning again to that major spokesman for both the industry and his company, we find Sir Henry enunciating the policy of both at The DCL annual meeting in September 1952. Sales policy, he declared, was 'governed by considerations of national interest and will so continue until we attain a stock position capable of meeting all demands'. Stocks of maturing Scotch had been 'considerably augmented during the year under review', he added with some pleasure. On sales policy in detail, he remarked, they aimed to sell a 'quality article at a reasonable price'. They could have got greater prices, but 'to have taken advantage of the temporary conditions would not have been in the long-term interests of the industry', while maintaining quality strengthened the reputation' of the brands. That is true of all established members of The SWA:

107

Sir Henry was, in effect, speaking not only as chairman of The DCL, but also as chairman of The Scotch Whisky Association.

On exports, Sir Henry summed up the industry's position: once more dollar markets were granted prior consideration and many other important markets had had to go short. On the other hand, they were still experiencing the general difficulties of world trade: Australia, for instance, had cut Scotch imports by 80 per cent; New Zealand had cut them by 20 per cent; South Africa was improving but all shipments to that market had to be carried out under licence. As to home sales, the 2.6 million gallons ration had been exceeded by about 40 per cent, as against 46 per cent the previous year.

Working now to a calendar year, in place of the Strachey/Webb year, it was finally agreed between the Ministry of Food, the Board of Trade and The SWA as 1952 drew to its close that in 1953 Scotch exports should be increased to 11 million proof gallons, an increase of 650,000 over 1952. Dollar markets were to continue to get priority but (the first gleam of liberalisation and freedom) exporters were to 'determine their remaining export markets according to their own views, both of short- and long-term commercial considerations'. This, more than seven years after the end of World War II and over thirteen years since its outbreak! For the home market, there was to be the diminutive increase of 150,000 gallons (1.25 million more bottles), the increase only being possible because of the improving stock position of mature whisky.

Some measure of real freedom came with the beginning of August 1953, when all orders controlling home-grown grains were abolished insofar as they affected the making of Scotch and gin. (The latter during war and post-war years had mostly relied on rectifying molasses spirit.) This meant the revocation of a number of orders including the Malt (Restriction) Order, 1940; Potable Spirits (Licensing and Control) Order, 1944; the Scotch Whisky (Auction Sales) Order, 1949. For Scotch, it was a great relief from a labyrinth of regulations and indicated just the possibility—no more—of an eventual return to comparatively free enterprise in the industry. But the concession was limited to home-grown grain, and prominent maltsters reported, 'No farmer wants to see the return of imported foreign barley for malting', drawing a contrast, in effect, with the sun-drenched barleys of California, Canada and Chile.

This August measure was hailed by the industry with the words that 'Whisky distillation may now be considered back to normal'. But this measure of freedom from control had little or no effect on immediate Scotch supplies. The whisky had to mature for a minimum of three years in the UK and in many other markets, and for a minimum of either four or five years in certain others. It was, however, a sign of the times, and a foretaste of the freedom yet to come.

Turning again to Sir Henry Ross, at the annual meeting in Edinburgh of The DCL the following month, September, we find him explaining that home sales in the 1952 calendar year were fixed at 2.6 million gallons, though actual releases to that market at 3.85 million were 48 per cent in excess, and for the 1953 calendar year the official allocation had been fixed at 2.75 million gallons. This again was expected to be outpaced by actuality.

On the export front, he was more expansive: the proportion of Scotch exported now far exceeded the amount drunk at home. Calls for shipments overseas, said Sir Henry, were 'still greater than the stocks we have available for release' and world distribution was still 'not altogether what we would desire'. His statement demands quotation, as typical of the industry in its last year of full government control:

We are still faced with problems and difficulties regarding exports to certain overseas markets. In some instances the extent of our trade is regulated by annual trade agreements in which specified import quotas are related to various UK exports. In others, such as Australia and South Africa, a limited amount of sterling

109

is made available to importers and our exports are restricted accordingly. This also applies to a number of markets in South America. The position, however, is such that any balances which we are unable to ship because of currency and other restrictions are readily taken up by other markets where no such difficulties exist.

He was satisfied that the policy of 'restriction of supplies within limits of availability of our adequately matured stocks is one which has undoubtedly enhanced the reputation of our brands in the markets of the world'. It was and has remained the policy of the industry as so represented.

There had been demands for doubling the price of Scotch to the USA, then rightly considered the wealthiest country on the globe. This was rejected: demand still exceeds supply, said Sir Henry, but 'the foothold of the industry in the US, although slowly growing firmer, is still slender in relation to the total volume of domestic and other whiskies consumed in that valuable market'. He went on: 'To trifle with such a delicate price structure would have a suicidal effect on our business', and Scotch whisky, he reminded the world, was Britain's 'largest single dollar-earning commodity'. The end of thraldom and the beginning of regained freedom were in sight.

Early in November 1953, The SWA announced that by agreement with the Ministry of Food the customary end-of-year discussions for settling the world pattern of distribution of Scotch would not be continued. Both government and industry took the view that the scheme of rationing and market priorities initiated in 1947 was no longer necessary, including the association's own scheme begun at home in 1940. Member firms were to be left free as from the beginning of 1954 to distribute their Scotches according to their own policy and resources—subject to an understanding to increase the rate of exports to the USA.

This was not meant to imply that Scotch was now in full and ample supply. Firms, it was pointed out, would still con-

110

tinue to limit their supplies to the home market and to various others abroad. Of equal importance, there would be no alteration in the scale of maximum prices laid down for the home market.

As The SWA had to announce the following month, December, all member firms must continue to enforce their own rationing schemes because 'the demand at home and abroad is too great for their supplies of mature whisky'. When the government agreement ended, the industry 'promised to do everything possible to continue enlarging its exports... [we] consider it imperative to rebuild the home market as quickly as possible, but will be hampered for some time to come because of the insufficiency of fully matured whisky to meet world demand'.

As Sir Henry put it at the spring meeting of The SWA in 1954, 1953 was 'a year of satisfaction' and with exports at 13.2 million proof gallons, home sales at 4.3 million gallons, to make a total of 17.5 million, it was, he said, 'the highest total in modern years'. He considered it, however, problematical whether 'a sufficient proportion of old whiskies to maintain or increase our sales in the coming year' existed in the industry's bonded warehouses.

Certainly those exports here referred to were the industry's greatest to that date, but it is common knowledge how they have gone on growing ever since—a growth restricted, at home, by excessive and repeated demands by Chancellors of the Exchequer of both political parties, and affected abroad from time to time in various markets by economic conditions prevailing within them.

But bearing in mind Edmund Burke's admonition that 'an ounce of arithmetic is worth more than a ton of rhetoric', we must just glance at some of the vital statistics of the years which led up to that measure of partial freedom at the end of 1953 and the beginning of 1954.

First, and most important, production and stocks in bonded

warehouses. In the distilling years ended 30 September, the outputs of Scotch were as follows: 1949, 27.7 million proof gallons; 1950, 29.2 million; 1951, 27.1 million; 1952, 30.1 million; 1953, 26.2 million; 1954, 32.8 million. Stocks grew accordingly, what with mounting production and careful rationing of matured whisky in bond. Stocks of Scotch had touched their depth, it will be remembered, by 31 March 1947, when there were only 79.9 million original proof gallons. Taking the same date throughout they rose in this fashion: 1948, 86.7 million original proof gallons; 1949, 98.9 million; 1950, 111.7 million; 1951, 124.1 million; 1952, 136.7 million; 1953, 148.5 million; 1954, 152.3 million.

The worst was over, but still rationing had to continue, quite apart from economic and political factors. And while export markets were the first to regain freedom from rationing and quotas, the home market was still continuing to be rationed until the spring of 1959 for the standard brands and into the 1960s for the older, more exclusive and de luxe brands.

But taking those closing years of control on a calendar year evaluation, the gradual freeing of exports worldwide and to the US emerges as follows: in 1950, world exports amounted to 9,708,000 proof gallons worth £23,326,000 ($55,982,400), the US share being 5,846,000 gallons valued at £16,761,000 ($40,226,400). In 1951, the world took 10,628,000 gallons costing £29,598,000 ($71,035,200), of which 6,111,000 gallons at £17,922,000 ($43,012,800), went to the US. In 1952 world exports totalled 11,531,000 gallons worth £33,039,000 ($79,293,600), while those to the US amounted to 6,301,000 gallons costed at £18,481,000 ($44,354,400). The year 1953 saw the world total at 13,202,000 gallons worth £37,768,000 ($90,643,200), the US share being 7,164,000 gallons valued at £20,782,000 ($49,876,800), and in 1954, the first year of 'freedom', world exports totalled 13,691,000 gallons priced at £39,055,000 ($93,732,000), of which shipments to the

US amounted to 7,131,000 gallons valued at £20,885,000 ($50,124,000).

As to home consumption of Scotch it reached its lowest depth ever in the year ending 31 March 1949, when it amounted to only 2.5 million gallons. Despite strict rationing by The SWA and member firms in 1950 it managed to grow to just 3 million gallons; in 1951, the year of the centenary of the great 1851 exhibition, it reached 3.8 million gallons. It sank back slightly in the 1952 year to 3.5 million, and only clambered to 3.9 million gallons in the 1953 year. But in anticipation of and as a result of the January 1954 'liberation', home sales of Scotch in the financial year ending 31 March 1954 reached 4.3 million gallons.

A few percentages may here be of interest. In the 1938-9 year, out of total world sales at home and abroad home sales accounted for 47.2 per cent of the total, and overseas sales to 52.8 per cent. In the 1952-3 year the percentages were: home, 24.9; overseas, 75.1. In 1953-4 they were: home, 24.4; overseas, 75.6 per cent of total world sales.

The industry, then, achieved some measure of freedom, freedom from excessive governmental control, beginning with 1954, but its expansion was still curtailed. Scotch is not a spirit that is distilled today and sold tomorrow. Between its creation and distribution lies a long span of years. Thus, without tracing expansion and progress year by year, it is enough to say that the industry did not manage to gain its freedom from quotas and rations for markets until 1959.

Just a few figures to indicate its growth since that 1954 freedom. In the distilling year October 1953–September 1954, Scotch output was 34.2 million original proof gallons. In the 1959-60 year it was 69.7 million gallons. In the 1964-5 year it amounted to 135.2 million gallons, and in 1970-1 soared to 147.5 million gallons, increasing in 1971-2 to 159 million gallons.

Stocks of Scotch maturing in their warehouses the length

and breadth of the land reflect that tremendous rise in output. At the end of September 1954, stocks totalled 157.9 million original proof gallons. By the end of the 1959-60 distilling year they had risen to 277,850,000 such gallons. At the end of the distilling year 1964-5 they amounted to 501 million gallons, and after the 1969-70 year to 787.8 million gallons. Moreover, it has been reliably estimated that at the end of the British financial year 1971-2 Scotch stocks amounted to 870 million gallons.

Taking that financial year, ending 31 March, as the unit, we find this pattern. In the 1953-4 year, 4.3 million proof gallons were taxpaid in the UK, and 13.3 million exported, a ratio of 24.5 per cent for the UK and 75.5 per cent for overseas. In 1959-60 the UK taxpaid 6.6 million gallons, and 22.7 million were exported, a ratio of 22.9 and 77.1 per cent. In the 1964-5 year 9.6 million gallons were drunk in the UK and 36.4 million exported, a ratio of 17.1 and 82.9 per cent. In 1969-70, 9.6 million gallons were taxpaid in Britain and 57.2 million exported, a ratio of 14.4 and 85.6 per cent. In the 1971-2 year it is calculated that 11.4 million gallons were taxpaid in the UK, and 70 million exported, a ratio of 13 and 87 per cent.

After that careful husbanding of maturing stocks in the 1950s, the industry entered the 1960s intent on a building boom, building its world sales with renewed energy, rebuilding its home market after twenty years of rationing, and building and enlarging distilleries, warehouses, and blending and bottling plants. That rebuilding of the home market was watched with a jealous eye by spendthrift Chancellors of the Exchequer who thought that Scotch sales at home had no right to surpass the pre-war level. So in July 1961, Chancellor Selwyn Lloyd increased the UK tax on Scotch by 10 per cent making it 231s 11d ($27.80) the proof gallon. In April 1964, Chancellor Maudling increased it to 257s 6d ($30.90) the gallon. A year later Chancellor Callaghan made it 292s ($34), and in July 1966 it underwent yet another 10 per cent increase to become 321s 4d ($38.60) a gallon. In March 1968, Chancellor Jenkins added again to the tax making it 342s 9d ($41.10) the proof gallon or £2 ($4.80) per bottle at 70° proof in the UK, and the following November yet another 10 per cent was added making it 377s ($45.25), or £2.20 ($5.30) per standard bottle. Such is the price of popularity. And it is significant that over-taxed as it is at home, Scotch sells as well as it does.

The danger, as leaders quoted earlier have said, is that this high rate of taxation in its country of origin leads importing countries around the world to copy the example of the British Government and increase their taxes on Scotch. Many have, on their own admission, done just that, and it's part of the success saga of Scotch that despite these high rates of taxation at home and abroad it still sells as well as it does. In the calendar year 1972 68,752,000 proof gallons valued at £227,912,000 were exported, and 12,595,000 proof gallons were taxpaid in the UK (estimated).

The reader is referred to the appendices (pp176-7) for details of some leading markets and their Scotch imports.

◈ 5 ◈

Stories about Scotch

'There are two things that a Highlander likes naked, and one of them is malt whisky,' runs the old saying in the north. Scotch whisky has so long been interwoven with the history of the land and people that it is impossible to put a date to many of the legends and anecdotes with which it is surrounded.

In the Highlands in particular, whisky was the great, the universal cure, the elixir proclaimed by the Mediterranean innovators of distillation. 'They administer it,' wrote a wandering eighteenth-century traveller, 'in colds, fevers, and faintings, and it is a frequent prayer of theirs that "God may keep them from that disorder that whisky will not cure".' Their practical faith in it was, indeed, such that it often resulted in overdosing, calling for a holiday in the country where the cure-all could be even more effectively repeated.

The first liquid imparted to a baby was a sip of whisky, and as one writer records about the Hebrides: 'The newly weds were expected to sit up in bed to receive their guests; whisky was passed round, and to end the proceedings one of the company threw two glassfuls of it in the faces of the bride and bridegroom.' The visitors then withdrew.

So intimately, then, was Scotland's national spirit associated with the strands of daily life, in birth, mating, and, as we shall see, in death. But for all that an exciseman wrote in

1736 about this devotion (or addiction) to Scotch whisky: 'The ruddy complexions, nimbleness, and strength of these people' —that is, the Highlanders—'is not owing to water-drinking, but to the aqua vitae, a malt spirit commonly used in that country, which serves both for victual and drink.'

How much so is further illustrated by a letter written a few years later, in December 1747, by Lt-Col Watson from Fort Augustus about the establishment of military stations in the north: 'How soon the posts are fixed the commanding officer at each station is to endeavour to ingratiate himself in the favour of some person in his neighbourhood by giving him a reward, or filling him drunk with whisky as often as he may judge proper, which I'm confident is the only way to penetrate the secrets of these people.'

Scotch-soaked funerals persisted into the last century, as witnessed by the *New Statistical Account*, 1843, quoted by Alasdair Alpine MacGregor in his *Skye and the Inner Hebrides* (1953), where the 'drinking of ardent spirits at funerals' was described as a 'lamentable feature' of social life in 1843. Poor families parted with their last horse or cow for funeral refreshments and 'thus what might have contributed to their support for a twelvemonth is wasted in a day, to keep up a savage and destroying custom'. MacGregor continued:

At many a funeral in the western Highlands and Islands the providing of a copious supply of whisky is still deemed a matter of prime honour, and one which the natives of Tiree observed to the full until very recently. On Tiree, nowadays, there is no halting between the deceased's house and the place of interment. Yet it is not long so since there were many, at each of which the funeral party indulged in a few rounds of the Best Scotch. A halt used to be made on the slightest pretext. Undue weariness of foot occasioned many a dram! ...

When all is in order, a brief committal service is held—*brief* it certainly had to be, because by this time the cart conveying the refreshments had arrived on the scene, and the mourners were drouthy with their exertions! Biscuits and cheese were then distributed, and drams freely dispensed. The greater the num-

117

ber of rounds, the greater the honour the natives believed they were paying to the dead.

The mourners' homeward journey was often boisterous and hilarious. Not infrequently, the least sober of them was literally *carted* home in the horse-drawn vehicle that had brought the whisky to the scene of their revels. There was a day—and not so long ago either—when more than one cart accompanied the procession, in order to carry home those defeated in brawling, and overcome in dramming.

A good story is told on Tiree of the way in which the natives often vied one with the other in the quantity of alcohol consumed at their funerals. When X's wife died, she was honoured with eleven drams. Shortly afterwards, X's son returned home from a funeral at a neighbouring township with the disconcerting tidings that thirteen drams had been given. This so annoyed his father that he threatened to dig his wife up, 'and we'll have fourteen rounds!'

More generally, MacGregor wrote that

where the dramming at funerals is concerned, that it had some connection with an ancient ritual into which seven, the mystical number, entered. Seven drams were given before setting out with the corpse, seven each time the bearers halted with it, and seven at the graveside. Two other occasions are regarded by the West Highlander [and not only by him] as justifying the most liberal consumption of intoxicants—the celebrating of the New Year, and a marriage. The pagan tradition that there must be plenty to drink at marriages and funerals, and on New Year's Day, is dying hard in these parts.

Just how deeply the drinking of Scotch whisky penetrated the daily life of the people is amply illustrated by the following excerpts. First, Morewood tells us in the second edition of his *Inebriating Liquors* (1838):

In the Western Islands, many of the customs of the ancient Caledonians and Britons are still preserved, and, amongst others, the old manner of drinking. In former times, large companies assembled, composed principally of the chief respectable men of the islands. This assemblage was called a *sheate, streah,* or *round,* from the company always sitting in a circle. The cup-bearer handed about the liquor in full goblets or shells, which the guests continued to drink until not a drop remained. This lasted for a day at least, and sometimes for two days . . .

During the revel, two men stood at the banqueting door with a barrow, and when anyone became incapable, he was carried to his bed, and they returned to dispose of the others in the same way. Sir Walter Scott, in a note to *The Lord of the Isles*, states that this custom was still in existence, and relates the anecdote of a gentleman of temperate habits, who, forming one of a company of this description, although permitted to remain neutral, was obliged to submit to the ceremony. Martin, in his *History of the Western Isles*, says it was deemed a breach of hospitality among persons of distinction to broach a cask of *aqua vitae*, and not see it finished at the time...

This drinking whisky from goblets or shells recalls the experience of Johnson and Boswell in their 1773 jaunt through Scotland and the Hebrides. 'We were entertained here with a primitive heartiness,' wrote Boswell about the Isle of Coll. 'Whisky was served round in a shell, according to the ancient Highland custom. Dr Johnson would not partake of it; but, being desirous to do honour to the modes "of other times", drank some water out of the shell.'

So deeply was Scotch embedded in the daily life of Scotland that as early as 1723 when the Society of Improvers of Agriculture in Scotland was formed at Edinburgh, embracing not only the leading nobility and gentry in Scotland but also tenant farmers, and, ultimately, gardeners, the objects included not only the cultivation of the land, the planting of trees and the rotation of crops but also the distilling of whisky. For whisky and farming had in their origins at least partly sprung from the same source: the cultivation of the land, the harvesting of the fruits of the earth.

In the transactions of the society is a letter addressed to a Mr Groat, of Warse in Caithness, and forwarded by him to the society, containing questions about the best mode of distilling. From the letter it would seem that the process was little understood and practised imperfectly. One writer reminds Groat of former conversations in which he had lamented 'the pernicious consequences of smuggling foreign brandy' which 'drained this country of its coin through money being sent to the French and the Dutch, who took none of our goods in return'. It was agreed that distilling from their own malted barley would tend to diminish smuggling, by making less demand for French and Dutch liquor to which 'Caithness and Orkney counties were notoriously addicted'.

More practically, 'an advantage to landlords and tenants was expected also from the increased demand for beer [barley] which was apt to get low in price'. In answer to the questions, minute directions were given for distilling and rectifying aqua vitae, which seems to have been much made in private houses and farmsteads. Those who made their own were told to let their spirits be 'well cooled' before using them 'because all new distilled spirits drink harsh'. The material part of the answers and directions were given on this occasion by a Mr Henricus van Wyndaerden, 'who came from Holland... settled in Edinburgh and followed the distilling business with success and a fair character, and helped to spirit up most of the distilleries we now have to follow that business'.

All this was a large contributory factor to the distilling success of the Lowland distillers, in particular of the Steins and their relatives the Haigs, in Fife and around Edinburgh. In turn it led to their supplying lots of mass-produced whisky to London gin-rectifiers; and this was a major motive for the attempted reform by Pitt the Younger, in 1784 and onwards, of the notorious Book of Rates dating back to 1660 and amended, revised and added to almost every year so that it was a veritable taxation jungle, affecting in particular spirit-producers and importers. This in turn gave rise to the classic period of Scottish tales, mythologies and legends about Scotch distilling.

Bridging the gap and slightly overlapping the period are those two exemplars of Scottish genius at verse, play and drinking, Robert Fergusson and Robert Burns.

First, from Fergusson's *Leith Races:*

120

> To whisky plooks that brunt for wooks
> On town-guard soldiers' faces,
> Their barber bauld his whittle crooks,
> An' scrapes them for the races ...

And from his *The Sitting of the Sessions:*

> Weel lo'es me o' you, business, now;
> For ye'll weet mony a drouthy mou';
> That's lang a eisning game for you.
> Withouten fill
> O' dribbles frae the gude brown cow,
> Or Highland gill.
>
> Rob Gibb's grey gizz, new frizzl'd fine,
> Will white as one snaw-ba' shine;
> Weel does he lo'e the lawen coin
> When dossied down,
> For whisky gills or dribs of wine
> In cauld forenoon.

Robert Burns is not only the national poet of Scotland, but also of Scotch, and a re-reading of his works is recommended. Two quotes must here suffice as tribute to his devotion to Scotch (malt) whisky and his testimony to it as being in his time the national drink of Scotland.

First, from *The Holy Fair:*

> Be't whisky gill, or penny wheep,
> Or ony stronger potion,
> It never fails, on drinkin' deep,
> To kittle up our notion
> By night or day.

And on the closure of the Ferintosh distillery of Forbes of Culloden:

> Thae curst horse-leeches o' th' Excise,
> Wha mak the whisky stells their prize—
> Haud up thy hand, deil! Ance—twice—thrice!
> There, seize the blinkers!
> An' bake them up in brunstane pies
> For poor damn'd drinkers

Ferintosh, the 'ancient brewery of aquavity in Cromarty',

H

is the first mention of a famous individual distillery and its whisky. Duncan Forbes, Whig jurist and politician, 'suffered the loss of his brewery of aqua vitae by fire in his absence' during the Revolution of 1688. As compensation, the Scots' Parliament in 1695 granted the family, in partial settlement of the damages they had sustained, the privilege of distilling taxfree their own aqua vitae from barley grown on their own lands. The concession was later amended and with the reforms of Pitt the Younger in 1784 was withdrawn altogether, but with £21,000 compensation.

Those reforms of spirits' taxation laws and regulations initiated by Pitt the Younger in 1784 opened up the floodgates of illicit distilling (usually referred to as smuggling), founded the whole substructure of the legends of Scotch, and secured the most valuable sites, still in use today, for the establishment of pot-still distilleries in the Highlands and Islands. The reference to smuggling is because when the Highlanders had to fetch provisions from the Lowlands they usually formed themselves into bands and set off with a hundred little ponies. Lacking money, they took with them their own form of gold—small kegs of whisky made in Highland bothies, on their farms, in inaccessible glens, to use as barter. As the government tried to stop or curtail their centuries' old practice of family distilling, the Highlanders moved into secret recesses of the mountains and smuggled their whisky to the towns.

As Barnard put it in his *Whisky Distilleries of the United Kingdom* (1887):

Both in Scotland and Ireland the smugglers may be looked upon as the pioneers of the Whisky trade. To them is largely due the superior quality of the Fine Old Malt Whisky that is made in these days, and the 'Sma' Stills', and 'Illicit Potheen' may be said to be the foundations upon which the vast Whisky Distilling interests were founded . . .

They may be looked upon as the pioneers of the Whisky Trade; no men understood better the localities where they could turn out good spirit, and this fact may be seen to this day, when we find many of the oldest distilleries existing upon sites which have been well known to have been chosen by smugglers of old as places where the purest mountain streams, flowing over moss and peats, could be used to distil and produce spirits of the finest descriptions.

The most famous of these locations and pioneers is, of course, Glenlivet—the glen of the Livet, running its nine-mile course to the river Aven—where there were some 200 smugglers, one of whom, George Smith, decided in 1824 after the rationalisation of the distillery laws to become a legal, licensed distiller.

As the old rhyme has it:

> Glenlivet it has castles three
> Drumin, Blairfindy, and Deskie,
> And also one distillery
> More famous than the castles three.

And as W. E. Aytoun put it in *The Massacre of Macpherson*:

> Fharson had a son,
> Who married Noah's daughter,
> And nearly spoiled ta Flood,
> By trinking up ta water:
>
> Which he would have done,
> I at least pelieve it,
> Had the mixture peen
> Only half Glenlivet.

Or as James Hogg, the Ettrick Shepherd, put it to 'Christopher North':

Gie me the real Glenlivet, and I weel believe I could mak' drinking toddy oot o' sea-water. The human mind naver tires o' Glenlivet, any mair than o' caller air. If a body could just find oot the exac' proportions and quantity that ought to be drunk every day, and keep to that, I verily trow that he might leeve for ever, without dying at a', and that doctors and kirkyards would go oot o' fashion.

The paeans of praise of The Glenlivet malt whisky are almost endless, but when George Smith in 1824 turned from being an illicit distiller to being a legal one he was regarded as a blackleg by his former smuggler friends. For years he went, literally, in peril of his life, with the constant risk of his distillery being destroyed by the smugglers. Their point of view is quite comprehensible: they were and had been for generations free, independent Scots who were not going to be restricted, enslaved, deprived of their ancient liberties of person and practice by politicians in Westminster, London.

A glance at a few distilleries, some now abandoned, most still active, at once reveals the old smuggler links. Tambowie distillery, for instance, by Milngavie, Dunbartonshire, in the heart of Rob Roy country, was located on the site of smugglers' distilling, and the cave cut out of rock where they carried out operations was converted into a store-room. The water used, straight from Tambowie Hills, was exactly the same as that used by the smugglers.

More entrancing is the story of the origin of Lagavulin distillery on the Isle of Islay, as told by Barnard:

> Lagavulin is said to be one of the oldest distilleries in Islay, the business to a certain extent having been founded in 1742.
>
> At that period it consisted of ten small and separate smuggling bothys for the manufacture of 'moonlight', which when working presented anything but a true picture of 'still life', and were all subsequently absorbed into one establishment, the whole work not making more than a few thousand gallons per annum ... Up to a century ago smuggling was the chief employment of crofters and fishermen, more especially during the winter, and many were the encounters which took place between them and the Government officers. Up to the year 1821 smuggling was a lucrative trade in Islay, and large families were supported by it. In those days every smuggler could clear at least ten shillings a day, and keep a horse and cow. Early in the century the buildings were converted into a legal Distillery ...

(Today, there are eight legal distilleries on Islay, capable of making over five million proof gallons of whisky.)

Perhaps the most famous of smuggler-distillery associations

is, however, perpetuated to this day at Highland Park distillery, at Kirkwall in the Orkneys. Highland Park malt whisky is generally reckoned one of the three best malt whiskies made in Scotland and in a sense it all goes back to a great and notorious smuggler of days long gone. Many are the stories of this smuggler, Magnus Eunson, and his band, and we must be content with this excerpt from Barnard:

> The site whereon the distillery now stands was the place where the famous Magnus Eunson carried on his operations. This man was the greatest and most accomplished smuggler in Orkney. By profession he was a UP Church Officer, and kept a stock of illicit whisky under the pulpit, but in reality he was a 'non Professing' distiller. This godly person was accustomed to give out the psalms in a more unctuous manner than usual if the excise officers were in church, as he knew that he was suspected, and that a party of revenue officers, taking advantage of his absence, might at that moment be searching his house.
>
> A singular story is told of this man. Hearing that the church was to be searched for whisky by a new party of excisemen, Eunson had all the kegs removed to his house, placed in the middle of an empty room, and covered with a clean white cloth. As the officers approached after their unsuccessful search in the church, Eunson gathered all his people, including the maid-servants, round the whisky, which, with its covering of white, under which a coffin lid had been placed, looked like a bier. Eunson knelt at the head with the Bible in his hand and the others with their psalm books. As the door opened they set up a wail for the dead, and Eunson made a sign to the officers that it was a death, and one of the attendants whispered 'smallpox'. Immediately the officer and his men made off as fast as they could, and left the smuggler for some time in peace.

Magnus was more fortunate than another smuggler whose story has come my way. John Dearg was both smuggler-distiller and middleman and at the time in question had large stocks awaiting shipment to Invergordon. Excise officers were searching the region and were expected at Dearg's place any moment. Dearg therefore got a tailor who often worked at the house to be laid out on the table as a corpse—with a bull of malt as a reward. The tailor agreed; he was covered with a sheet, and the lamentation began. As the knock on the door echoed through the house—the knock of the officers—the tailor blackmailed Dearg into two bolls of malt, under threat of disclosure of the deceit. The officers withdrew from the house of mourning and the 'dead brother', to learn later that Dearg never had a brother.

To revert to the smuggler-inspired location of these malt distilleries. Miltonduff-Glenlivet distillery, near Elgin, in the Glen of Pluscarden, had as many as fifty illicit distillers as predecessors, and the smugglers continued their operations well into the last century although Miltonduff distillery itself was an early (1824) foundation as a legal plant. So favoured a spot was the Glen of Pluscarden by the smugglers that they invented a signalling system of their own. Three hills formed a triangle to enclose the whole area, and when an excise officer appeared a flag was hoisted on one of the hills as a warning to all. But it so happened that an energetic officer lay in wait all night and when the men were in the fields the next morning he approached the suspected house. Mrs Watson, the guidwife, was a large and muscular woman. The officer was of a somewhat smaller build. Opening the door he discovered in the room all the utensils of the previous night's distilling and the browst, or brewing.

'Aye, Mrs Watson, I have clean caught you this morning,' he said.

'Oh, aye,' she replied in a whisper. 'Did anybody see ye come in?'

'No,' he answered.

Rolling up her sleeves, she retorted, 'And, by the lord Harry, naebody will ever see ye gang oot!'

The officer disappeared forever from Pluscarden. He was succeeded by a man as wise as a serpent and harmless as a dove. When he intended to give the residents a visit, due warning was discreetly conveyed, and, no doubt, this thoughtful officer sampled the various local distillings on his rounds.

Balmenach distillery, in the Glenlivet district of Strathspey, gives us a prize example of the smugglers' choice of site. In Barnard's words: 'The range of the Cromdale Hills, some seven or eight miles long, stretched out before us. In days gone by these acclivities were the favourite haunts of smugglers, who chose the locality on account of the numerous hill-streams, whose waters are of fine quality and highly suitable for distilling purposes.'

Barnard and party, led by the proprietor's son, McGregor Junior, visited the smugglers' haunts:

He first directed us to the double-arched cavern, dug deep in the hill, fifty yards from the Distillery, in which at one time a noted band of smugglers carried out their operations... It possessed an underground spring, wherein the little coil of worm, which condensed the precious spirit, was laid, and at a lower level it dripped into a receiver, made out of an earthern jar some two feet high, with a wooden lid thereon. The little copper Still stood on a furnace made with the loose stones that had fallen from the rock behind, and the Mash-tun had originally been a wash-tub. The place was totally dark, and no light was ever permitted except that which came from the furnace fire.

One night the Revenue Officers made a raid on the place, and knowing the desperate men they had to deal with, were all well armed. On their arrival they crept stealthily through the narrow entrance to the cave, following the informer, who knew the place well. Meanwhile the smugglers, unconscious of the close proximity of their enemies, were scattered about the cavern, some sleeping, other smoking, and one or two looking after the distilling operations.

One of their number opened the furnace door to replenish the fire, and the momentary flash of light revealed to his comrade the figures of the officers stealing upon them. With great presence of mind he instantly unhooked the pipe which connected the furnace with a concealed chimney in the roof, and then fired off his pistol at the nearest enemy. The noise alarmed the gang who escaped from the cave, under cover of the dense smoke emitted from the open furnace. The officers were dumbfounded, and almost choked, but the informer quickly replaced the chimney-pipe, and as soon as the smoke had dispersed, the officers lighted their lamps from the furnace fire, and proceeded to demolish the place...

127

This scare broke up and scattered the notorious gang, and since that time there has been very little smuggling in this district.

Barnard's visit to Aberfeldy, Perthshire, also brought to light the earlier smugglers' exploits and their use of caves. He wrote of the visit:

In olden days the whole of this district abounded with smugglers' bothies. Our loquacious driver was the grandson of a notorious smuggler, and pointed out to us as we passed a farm-house perched on the top of a hill, which was the scene of the smuggler's nefarious practices. On the face of this hill, and just under the farm-house kitchen, was a spacious cave, entered by a small opening made by a dried-up water-course. This they blocked up with stones and pieces of rock, leaving an opening of a few inches wide for the water to trickle through from a spring, which they diverted from the other side of the hill, and brought through the cave. They then burrowed an entrance from a distant thicket, for ingress and egress, and carried a flue from the furnaces some seventy yards underground to the farm-house chimney. Here for years they made whisky, while their confederates lived in the farm-house pretending to till the land, but always on guard.

In an evil day for them, one of their number, out of revenge, peached to the Revenue Officers, who made a raid upon the place in the middle of the night, broke up the still, tubs, and worm, and took away a few kegs of whisky. Three only of the smugglers were at work at the time, who were just making up the furnace fire for the night, when a comrade rushed in and informed them that the officers of justice were close upon them.

However, as the night was very dark, all four managed to escape, and fled to America...

The stories are endless, and embrace not only the best distillery sites, but, like Scotch itself, every aspect of life. This one recorded by Barnard in 1886 is typical, and relates to Campbeltown:

A capital story is told of an aged woman who resided near Hazelburn [distillery]. She was of a rather doubtful character and was charged before the Sheriff with smuggling. The charge being held proven, it fell to his lordship to pronounce sentence. When about to do so he thus addressed the culprit, 'I dare say my poor woman it is not often you have been guilty of this fault.' 'Deed no Sheriff,' she readily replied, 'I haena made a drap since youn wee keg I sent to yersel.'

Barnard also recounts a smuggler's tale with a happier ending in Perthshire:

The burns...fall into the Tay, and are associated at every secluded bend and shady corner with the smuggling bothy, where illicit distillation was carried on extensively in olden times. Among the Strath Tay smugglers there were men of remarkable muscular power and shrewd audacity.

A surviving remnant of the brotherhood...still tells of a halloween night some forty years ago, when the famous Stewart arrived at a place near Perth with a boatload of potheen. He had sent up to the town for assistance to remove the Whisky, when 'lo and behold!' instead of his friends, the revenue officers appeared on the scene. Stewart immediately rowed out to midstream, but the officers seeing an idle boat followed him. A chase commenced, and the smuggler seeing that he was closely pressed, and that capture seemed inevitable, proceeded to use strategy that he might escape out of their clutches.

Pretending to surrender, he invited the gaugers into his boat to take possession, and seized one of their oars to assist them in stepping on board. In a twinkle he had thrown the oar on the top of his potheen barrels, and quickly rowed down the stream, leaving the poor discomforted gaugers with but one oar 'to paddle their own canoe' as best they could. He was soon lost to sight, and landed his cargo safely in one of his hiding places on the river-side.

The career of this noted smuggler is a record of unbroken triumph; his last distillation was sold in Leith, and was conveyed thither in a canopied cart, containing a caretaker muffled up as a patient (with an infectious disease), who managed thus to escape the prying curiosity of the exciseman, and succeeded in disposing of the Whisky at a high price.

Aultmore distillery, near Keith, is located in a setting once famous for four smugglers' bothies. The bothy near Auchinderran carried on by one Jane Milne used the same water as that now used by the legal distillery.

On one occasion [runs the local story] an old crofter was caught by a preventive officer while conveying the product with his pony and cart to one of the neighbouring towns. The officer, to make sure of his capture, led the pony along the road to a convenient place where he could confiscate the goods, the old smuggler at the same time keeping up a steady flow with the preventive. Only a short distance along the road had been covered when the neighbours, observing the old man's plight, stole up behind the cart and removed the jars containing the spirit, leaving nothing for the officer to confiscate.

The outlying districts were visited from time to time by the preventive men in search of smugglers, and, when one was known to be in the district, a white cloth about two yards square was placed on the peat stack as a warning to the neighbours. It was mostly in the winter season that the concealed spirit-making was carried on, and, to preserve the yeast between the brewing periods, the smuggler cut small birch bushes in foliage, saturated the leaves with yeast, then placed them in the old-fashioned hanging chimney to dry, the peat smoke preserving the yeast for further distilling.

One final tale of violence during the hey-day of smuggling. It concerns the Evanton district of Ross-shire and I draw this account from the *Inverness Courier*, April 1827:

> The previous week a party of Revenue men were compelled to retreat from Strathglass. They put up at a public house at Comar, and were warned that if they did not instantly return home, 'after what they had already destroyed', worse would happen to them. Mr Macniven, who was in charge of the party, disregarded the warning and next morning set forward. About two miles beyond the public house a smart fire commenced from the upper grounds, and on arriving in a narrow pass of the road, his further progress was stopped by about twenty men, armed with muskets and arrayed within gunshot. The Revenue party, consisting of ten men being armed only with pistols and short cutlasses, had no alternative but to retreat from the determined purpose of slaughter shown by the smugglers, and retired accordingly from the unequal contest; nor is it of any avail for the Revenue officers to attempt a seizure in that quarter until powerfully and efficiently armed.

Again, in 1835, the Strathglass violence was repeated: 'On Wednesday a party of the *Atlanta* Revenue cutter, consisting of an officer and four men, while discharging their duty in Strathglass, were attacked by a band of smugglers, about 14 in number, and driven back with great violence.'

Not all distilling was, however, illicit. Some plants sprang from the best of motives. To give but one instance: in 1819 the Marquis of Stafford, afterwards first Duke of Sutherland, founded Clynelish distillery by Brora in Sutherland. In a sense it was an early manifestation of the enclosure movement in the Highlands, but was done with the best of intentions. Until then the inhabitants of the county had lived in scattered hamlets in the interior but were gradually being moved down to nearer the coast, where allotments were provided for them. In order to provide a ready market for their barley from the newly cultivated land, the marquis founded the distillery. He chose the situation partly because of the nearness of the Brora coalfield, though this later came to be of no advantage as the coal was too poor to use at Clynelish as the century wore on. It became so famous and renowned a distillery, however, that by the end of the last century its product had to be rationed, both for blending and as a single malt whisky.

Elizabeth Grant of Rothiemurchus has left us wonderfully clear sketches of whisky-drinking in her day in her *Memoirs of a Highland Lady*. In this extract she is writing of 1812:

> The cheer she offered us was never more than bread and cheese and whisky... The whisky was a bad habit... At every house it was offered, at every house it must be tasted or offence would be given, so we were taught to believe... Whisky-drinking was and is the bane of that country; from early morn till late at night it went on. Decent gentlewomen began the day with a dram. In our house the bottle of whisky, with its accompaniment of a silver salver full of small glasses, was placed on the side-table with cold meat every morning. In the pantry a bottle of whisky was the allowance per day, with bread and cheese in any required quantity... The very poorest cottages could offer whisky; all the men engaged in the wood manufacture drank it in goblets three times a day, yet except at a merry-making we never saw any one tipsy.

(But she does remark a few pages later that 'temperance and chastity were not in the Highland code of morality'.)

She visited the 'Spey floaters'—they floated great logs down the river Spey—in 1813 and has left us this record of them and their whisky consumption:

> And there, after their hard day's work, they lay down for the night, in their wet clothes—for they had been perhaps hours in the

131

river—each man's feet to the fire, each man's plaid round his chest, a circle of wearied bodies half-stupified by whisky... They were a healthy race, suffering little except in their old age from rheumatism.

The men probably had their private dram before beginning the day, yet, on collecting [together] whisky was always handed round; a lad with a small cask—a quarter anker—on his back, and a horn cup in his hand that held a gill, appeared three times a day amongst them. They all took their 'morning' raw, undiluted and without accompaniment, so they did the gill at parting when the day was done; but the noontide dram was part of a meal. There was about 20 minutes' rest from labour, and a bannock and a bit of cheese taken out of every pocket to be eaten leisurely with the whisky. When we [the laird's family] were there the horn cup was offered first to us, and each of us took a sip to the health of our friends around us...

Sometimes a floater's wife or bairn would come up with a message; such messenger was always offered whisky. Aunt Mary had a story that one day a woman with a child in her arms, and another bit thing at her knee, came up among them; the horn cup was duly handed to her, she took a 'gey guid drap' herself, and then gave a little to each of the babies. 'My goodness, child,' said my mother to the wee thing that was trotting by the mother's side, 'doesn't it *bite* you?' 'Ay, but I like the bite,' replied the creature.

But the great and crowning glory of smuggler's Scotch came in 1822 with the first-ever visit of an Hanoverian monarch to Scotland, the visit of King George IV to Edinburgh. Elizabeth Grant tells the story:

The whole country went mad. Everybody stormed every point to get to Edinburgh to receive him. Sir Walter Scott and the Town Council were overwhelming themselves with preparations... One incident connected with this time made me very cross. Lord Conyngham, the Chamberlain, was looking everywhere for pure Glenlivet whisky; the King drank nothing else. It was not to be had out of the Highlands. [This was before George Smith's 1824 establishment of his distillery there, and when there were about 200 smugglers in the Glenlivet.]

My father sent word to me—I was the cellarer—to empty my pet bin, where was whisky long in wood, long in uncorked bottles, mild as milk, and the true contraband goût in it. Much as I grudged this treasure it made our fortunes afterwards, showing on what trifles great events depend. The whisky, and fifty brace of ptarmigan all shot by one man, went up to Holyrood House, and

were graciously received and made much of, and a reminder of
this attention at a proper moment by the gentlemanly Chamberlain ensured to my father the Indian judgeship...

As Burns said in his *Epitaph on John Dove*:

> Strong ale was ablution,
> Small beer, persecution,
> A dram was *momento mori*...

Lockhart has left us this account, in his *Life* of Scott, of the
arrival of George IV for 'the Royal Fortnight', of which Scott
was, in effect, Scottish stage-manager:

Sacrifice.

Good Templar. "Tut—t—t—Really, Swizzle, it's Disgraceful to see a Man in your Position in this State, after the
promise we've incurred and the exertions we've used to put down the Liquor Traffic!"

Swizzle. "Y' may Preash as mush as y' Like, Gen'l'm'n, but I can tell y' I've made more Persh'nal Efforsh to (*hic*)
down Liquor than any of ye!"

About noon on the 14th of August, the royal yacht and the attendant vessels of war cast anchor in the Roads of Leith... In the midst of the rain, however, Sir Walter rowed off to the *Royal George*, and, says the newspaper of the day, 'To this record let me add, that, on receiving the Poet on the quarter-deck, his Majesty called for a bottle of Highland whisky, and having drunk his health in this national liquor, desired a glass to be filled for him. Sir Walter, after draining his own bumper, made a request that the King would condescend to bestow on him the glass out of which his Majesty had just drunk his health...'

That the royal preference should be for the illicit malt whisky is of interest, for in April 1831 Major Cumming Bruce wrote to the *Inverness Courier*:

It is asserted that the rage for the use of whisky is still increasing, while to our sad experience we know that its quality is deteriorating among us. It is no longer the pure dew of the mountain which issued from the bothies of our free traders of the hills, healthful and as exhilarating as the drops which the sun's first rays drink up from the heathbell of the Cairngorms, but a vile, rascally, mixed compotation which fires the blood and maddens the veins without warming the heart, or, like the old, elevating the understanding.

We will end this chapter with another royal occasion, that when Queen Victoria visited John Begg's distillery sited within a mile of Balmoral Castle. Begg held the lease of the property under the queen. The event was in 1848, and Begg recorded it thus in his journal:

I wrote a note on the 11th September to Mr G. E. Anson [Her Majesty's Private Secretary] stating that the distillery was now in full operation, and would be so until six o'clock next day, and, knowing how anxious HRH Prince Albert was to patronize and make himself acquainted with everything of a mechanical nature, I said I should feel much pleasure in showing him the works. The note was handed in at Balmoral Castle about 9 pm. Next day about four o'clock, whilst in the house, I observed Her Majesty and the Prince Consort approaching. I ran and opened the door, when the Prince said, 'We have come to see through your works Mr Begg.' There were besides, TRH the Prince of Wales, the Princess Royal, and Prince Alfred, accompanied by Lady Cumming. I at once conducted the Royal Party to the distillery.

134

On entering the works, the two young Princes at once ran away among the casks, like any other children, whereupon Her Majesty called them, 'Where are you young children going?' on which I laid hold of one in each hand, and held them during the time they remained.

I endeavoured to explain the whole process of malting, brewing and distilling, showing the Royal Party the bere [barley] in its original state, and in all its different stages of manufacture until it came out at the mouth of the still pipe in spirits. HRH tasted the spirits with his finger from both the still pipes. On going downstairs HRH turned round to me and said (looking at the locks on the stills), 'I see you have got your locks there.' On my replying, 'These are the Queen's locks', Her Majesty took a hearty laugh.

When we came to the door I asked HRH if he would like to taste the spirit in its matured state, as we had cleared some that day from bond, which I thought was very fine. HRH having agreed to this, I called for a bottle and glasses (which had been previously in readiness) and, presenting one glass to Her Majesty, she tasted it. So also did His Royal Highness the Prince. I then presented a glass to the Princess Royal, and to the Prince of Wales, and Prince Alfred, all of whom tasted the spirit.

HRH the Prince of Wales was going to carry his glass quickly to his mouth. I checked him, saying it was very strong, so he did not take but a very small drop of it. Afterwards the Royal Party took their departure, I thanking them for the honour of the visit they had been so generous to pay the distillery.

Following the visit Begg was granted the right to call his distillery the Royal Lochnagar Distillery, and was also appointed by royal warrant distiller to the queen.

On that royal note we must leave this all too brief collection of stories concerning that equally royal drink Scotch whisky, and turn to stories of another sort, courtroom stories and their consequences.

⚜ 6 ⚜

Scotch at Law

What is whisky? It seems a simple enough question which calls for an easy answer. But it took the authorities and the trade in Great Britain over a quarter of a century to define it, and it then took the British Government over forty years to pass a law defining Scotch whisky; and as late as the Finance Act of 1969 they still further defined it.

What sort of still can it be made in? What materials may be used in making it? Does it need to be matured? Can Scotch whisky be made only in Scotland? Can different sorts of whisky—allowing there are more sorts than one—be mixed or blended, and still be called whisky? What are the proportions to be used in the mixture/blend? These are just some of the questions which were posed with the startlingly rapid progress of the Scotch industry in the last twenty years of the nineteenth century.

We are accustomed today of speaking of malt whisky made in pot stills, and grain whisky made in patent stills. But it was by no means as simple or as generally accepted as that. The first rumblings of discontent began in the Highlands among the pot-still distillers of malt whisky who, with their ancestors, had mostly been making malt whisky in pot stills for generations. That alone, they considered, was whisky. When Andrew Usher's innovation of mixing, or blending, malt whisky made in the traditional manner with grain spirit made in the new-

136

fangled patent still—patented in 1831 it was regarded as a newcomer—began to spread, the traditionalists began to murmur and get angry at this theft of their name of whisky to the grain spirit.

'We shall perhaps tread on somebody's corn,' said a Highland distiller in May 1886, 'when we venture to say that Patent Grain Spirit is not "Whisky" as we and the majority of the trade understand it, any more than Berlin Spirit is Cognac Brandy, though figuring in combination with the latter very expensive article. One of these days the Trade may wake up to find more of us Scottish Highland distillers refusing to be dragged at the chariot-wheels of the all-pervading Patent Still, and going direct to the consumer.'

The point about cognac brandy was that because of the phylloxera vineyard scourge brandy-production was being reduced to near-nil, and various counterfeit substitutes were finding their way on to the market; counterfeits which led to prosecutions and ultimately to Scotch being put in the dock.

Feeling grew, and another big Scotch dealer went on record about these new-fangled blends of pot-still whisky and patent-still spirit, as it was still widely called: 'Fifteen to twenty years ago a "Blend" was regarded as applied only to Highland whisky, the strong individuality—now rare—of the produce of each still requiring assimilation. Now the word "Blend" has become a term of reproach in the Trade in consequence of its being applied to what were then known as "Mixtures".'

Just about this time the famous margarine cases came to a head. In many cases, where successful prosecutions were brought, margarine had been sold masquerading as butter, or sometimes 'butterine'. Offenders were prosecuted under Section 6 of the Sale of Food and Drugs Act, 1875—which played an important part in the Scotch story—which avoided the term 'adulteration' and gave a clearer definition of punishable offences. 'No person shall sell to the purchaser any article of food or any drug which is not of the nature, substance and quality of the article demanded by the purchaser under a penalty...'

An important phrase that: '...not of the nature, substance and quality demanded...' The whole question of whether grain spirit was entitled to be called grain whisky was to hang on just that legal phrase.

In 1887 the Margarine Act was passed, clearing up that counterfeit tangle, and word came from Elgin, the headquarters of the Highland pot-still distillers, as follows: 'The Northern Malt Distillers have lately determined to test the question whether it is not "adulteration" to put Grain spirit into Malt and dub the "blend" "Highland Whisky". If such a decision were obtained it would fall like a bombshell into the "Grain" market, and with the "butterine" question fresh in memory, we do not put such a decision out of the region of possibility.'

The minutes of the annual meeting in August 1887 of the North of Scotland Malt Distillers Association at Elgin record that: 'The attention of the Association was particularly directed against the adulteration of whisky, and, in order to secure the public against that practice, the meeting came to a resolution to apply to the Board to enforce the Adulteration Act. It was pointed out that this was a matter of the utmost importance, not only in the interests of the public, but in their own as Distillers of Malt Whisky. It was thought that by having a certified label, or such like, Whisky could be provided against adulteration in the same way as were milk and other goods.' (There had been a spate of cases against waterers of milk.)

If for no other reason, it was just about this time and in succeeding years that blenders began buying up or erecting their own malt-whisky distilleries: at least they could thus make sure of a proportion of their malt-whisky supplies, and even The Distillers Company Ltd, the biggest group of grain-spirit distillers, soon built their first Highland malt distillery, Knockdhu, in 1893-4.

Meanwhile, partly as a result of genuine concern about public health, partly because of Highland pressures, a Select Committee of the House of Commons was appointed in 1890 and reappointed the next year to consider 'whether, on grounds of public health, it is desirable that certain classes of spirits, British and foreign, should be kept in bond for a definite period ... and to inquire into the system of blending British and foreign spirits in or out of bond, and into the propriety of applying the Sale of Food and Drugs Acts and the Merchandise Marks Act to the case of British and foreign spirits and mixtures of British and foreign spirits, and also into the sale of ether as an intoxicant'.

As the committee put it, they were limited in their inquiries 'in regard to the bonding and blending of spirits, and to their effect on public health' and were 'empowered to consider whether the Merchandise Marks Act and the Food and Drugs Act should be extended to spirits so as to enable the public to know the character, origin, and state of purity of the products offered for consumption and to limit the sale when they are deleterious'.

Here was one of the problems facing the committee, in their own words:

There is no exact legal definition of spirits going by popular names, such as whisky, brandy, rum, patent or silent spirits. Some witnesses desire to define whiskey [the usual official spelling for years] as the spirit made in pot stills, and would deny that name to spirits made in patent stills, even though the proportion of malt and grain used in the production might be the same in both. Some of the distillers from malt desired that their whiskey should be called 'malt whiskey' though the general name 'whiskey' might be extended to those who mix malt with grain. On the other hand, certain distillers in Belfast and Scotland urged that spirits distilled in patent stills from malt and grain were entitled to be considered as whiskey; that they are used sometimes as such directly, and are now largely employed in blending pot still whiskey. They gave evidence that there was increased demand for a whiskey of a milder kind, and that blends of pot still and patent still whiskey were in large demand by the consumers, who thus obtained a cheaper and a milder whiskey containing a smaller quantity of fusel oil and other bye-products.

Your Committee do not attempt a legal definition of whiskey...

Whiskey is certainly a spirit consisting of alcohol and water, with a small quantity of bye-products coming from malt and grain, which give to it a peculiar taste and aroma. It may be diluted with water without ceasing to be whiskey, and it may be diluted with spirits containing little of the bye-products to suit the pocket and palate of customers, and it still goes by the popular name of whiskey. Your Committee are unable to restrict the use of the name as long as the spirits added are pure and contain no noxious ingredients...

Your Committee do not recommend any increased restrictions on blending spirits... The addition of patent still spirits, even when it contains a very small amount of bye-products, may be viewed rather as a dilution than an adulteration, and, as in the case of the addition of water, is a legal act within the limits of strength regulating the sale of spirits.

So much for definition and blending. On the question of a minimum age they reported:

Our general conclusion from the evidence submitted to us is, that compulsory bonding of all spirits for a certain period is unnecessary and would harass trade... As the public show a marked preference for old spirits, which the trade find more profitable, and as the practice has arisen of blending whiskeys with patent spirits, to fit them for earlier consumption, it is not desirable to pass any compulsory law in regard to age, especially as the general feeling of the trade is that such an obligation would harass commerce, and be an unfair burden...

There the matter rested, while the Scotch boom continued. But it should be noted that the committee seemed to make a distinction—strictly undefined—between whisky and patent-still spirits. They even specifically reported that 'various blends are made, either by the mixture of pot-still products, or by the addition of silent spirits from the patent stills'. This, and the whole report, rather suggested denying the name 'whisky' to patent-still spirits, rather contemptuously dubbed, in places, silent spirits because they were silent about their origin and 'parentage'.

140

Things lay dormant on the surface for a while, and then came a spate of cognac prosecutions under that Section 6 of the Sale of Food and Drugs Act in which so-called 'cognac brandy' had been sold to a customer which was 'not of the nature, substance and quality demanded'. These brought reactions on the Scotch whisky front, and in March 1904 Sir Herbert Maxwell, MP for Wigtown, introduced his Sale of Whisky Bill. Maxwell and fellow-promoters defined the object of the bill as being 'to secure to purchasers of whisky a clear statement whether it is made from barley malt alone, or is in part a spirit made from unmalted grains'. All casks and other vessels holding Scotch would have to be so marked, and the basic intention was to discredit grain whisky and clear the field for pot-still malt whisky. It got no farther than its first reading, but was accompanied by a brisk warfare of parliamentary questions alleging 'whisky frauds'. The questions all received stalling answers; the Parliament was nearing its end; private members' bills were swamping the House; the government wanted to end its days in peace and quiet undisturbed by squabbles, as they considered them, between distillers.

In mid-1904 Islington Borough Council, London, won a well publicised 'brandy' case in which the article sold as brandy was 'not of the nature, substance and quality demanded'. The *Lancet*, with brandy's medicinal virtues in mind, joined in the hue and cry, stating:

Brandy is spirit distilled from the fermented juice of the grape . . . There can be no disguising the fact that of recent years a large section of the spirit trade has adopted a method of business which has hoodwinked the public. Spirituous liquors, chiefly brandy and whisky, have been placed upon the market which were not accurately described by the labels upon the bottles.

We have pointed out again and again that the terms 'Brandy' and 'Whisky' had specified meanings, these terms being used to distinguish in the former case a spirit derived exclusively from wine and in the latter case a spirit derived from barley malt. We have been assured that the attenuation of genuine Brandy or

141

Whisky with a spirit made from grain, potatoes or other materials was the result of the demand made by the public in favour of a spirit of negative rather than positive characteristics.

It suited certain sections of the Trade to say this, while all the time they knew perfectly well that their real object was to put upon the market a cheaper spirit and to gain a wider margin of profit upon it. Whatever else may be said, such trading is not honest dealing with the public, apart altogether from the question of whether this or that spirit is more wholesome than the other ...

Such were the passions, the urgency of the issue at the time, that the sedate, specialist *Lancet* felt compelled to speak out in such language!

Squabbles, preachings and prosecutions of one sort or another went on, and in mid-1905 the US Government joined in. Harvey Wylie, of the US Bureau of Chemistry, toured Scottish and Irish distilleries to arrive at standards for Scotch and Irish blended whiskies so that the American buyer would know exactly what he was getting.

Islington Borough Council was girding up its loins for an attack on 'spurious' whiskies (Scotch and Irish) whiskies 'not of the nature, substance and quality demanded'. In short, were blended whiskies legally entitled to the name 'whisky'? A dozen charges were made against on- and off-licensees, and two selected as test cases. The famous 'What *is* whisky?' case began, and it was almost four years before it was settled.

On 6 November 1905, two licensees appeared before Mr E. Snow Fordham, stipendiary magistrate at the North London Police Court, Islington, charged with selling as whisky an 'article not of the nature, substance and quality demanded'. James Davidge, off-licensee of Hornsey Road, was charged in connection with Scotch, and Thomas Samuel Wells, on-licensee of Hornsey, in connection with Irish whiskey.

The Off-Licences Association could not afford to defend their members—they were out of funds after the brandy cases—and after various approaches and discussions the grain-whisky distillers decided to take up the defence of the cases.

142

The grain distillers saw their whole future threatened. It was felt that the case was simply another attempt by some malt-whisky distillers to get the better of the grain-whisky distillers by means of court action, as legislation and parliamentary questions and other tricks had failed.

With the grain distillers, headed by The Distillers Company Ltd, backing the cases, taking them over in effect, the North London Police Court saw a galaxy of legal and technical talent on parade. For the charges related simply to the fact that a blend of grain and malt whisky was not whisky. Or was it? The court decided it was not.

For interest's sake we may note that the bottle of 'Fine Old Scotch Whisky' bought from Davidge cost 2s 6d (30c), was made in June 1904, or possibly a year before as to 90 per cent of its contents, and contained less than 10 per cent malt whisky. Wells's was only one month old when received into his cellar in May and was all sold within six months; it was 90 per cent grain whisky, or spirit, as the prosecution charged. Price, 2s 4d (28c).

The case went on for weeks, intermittently, and Fordham gave his judgement on 26 February 1906. He was a pot-still malt-whisky man, and he found the charges proved of selling an 'article not of the nature, substance and quality demanded'. That is, patent-still spirit, or grain whisky, was *not* whisky; only pot-still spirit made from malt, or malt and grain in the case of Irish whiskey, was whisky.

A few quotes from Fordham are of more than passing interest:

Irish whiskey and Scotch whisky are just as much definite articles as Bourbon or Canadian whisky ... and I must hold that by Irish or Scotch whisky is now meant a spirit obtained in the same methods by the aid of the form of still known as the pot still. The product of the patent still cannot in itself be either Scotch whisky or Irish whiskey, although made in Ireland or Scotland ...

Now having found that the fluids sold by the defendants were spirits produced in a patent still from a mash consisting of maize, to which a dash of pot still had been added, I find that

143

Wells' sample is not Irish whiskey, and Davidge's sample is not Scotch, as was demanded by the purchasers.

Irish and Scotch whisky is one thing, and patent still spirit with a little whisky added is another ... But when a purchaser asks for and pays for whisky it should be given to him by the seller, or at any rate the purchaser should know what he is getting. Certainly if he is not getting what he asks for he is prejudiced. I find that both Wells and Davidge have infringed the law, and I must fix and order penalties in each of those two summonses ...

Patent still spirit, made largely from maize, has been sold as whisky in a largely increasing manner for years, and the resulting product has been taken by an unsuspecting public to the benefit of the wholesale dealers and retailers, and the so-called blenders have dared to concoct and place upon the market raw, new patent spirit with a mere dash of Irish or Scotch whisky in it as Irish and Scotch ...

In my opinion, the blenders who supplied the defendants should be the people to suffer, but at the same time in my judgement it was careless on the part of the defendants to sell it as they had done, and since they only are before me, they must pay the penalty for the infringement of the law ... I shall impose only a nominal fine of 20s, and £100 costs each; or in the alternative, two months' imprisonment in each division.

Was this the end of blending? Of grain whisky—or spirit? Notice of appeal was given at once. The grain distillers and blenders had too much at stake; their very existences were threatened.

Reduced to its logical conclusion, of course, Fordham's decision was anti-progressive; it meant that no improvement or change in distilling methods was possible or permissible; all whisky must be made in the most primitive fashion that could be discovered from ancient archives; the earliest records would have to be ransacked for evidence as to materials and methods first used.

As a result of Fordham's decision, Archibald Williamson, MP for Elgin and Nairn, the very heart of pot-still land, introduced another Sale of Whisky Bill with the object, so stated, of securing to purchasers a clear statement whether the whisky was pot-still malt whisky or malt and corn whisky, or in part patent-still and unmalted spirit. So, proposed the bill: 'All whisky shall, from the time of leaving the distillery till sold to the consumer, be described by a mark or label on the cask or bottle as "Whisky" or "Blend of Whisky and Patent Still Spirit", as the case may be. Provision is made for similar information being given to persons purchasing whisky on draught.'

Williamson's bill was revived in the spring of 1907 but never saw the statute book; it is mentioned here simply as indicative of the temper of the times. In the spring of 1906, just after Fordham, Aberdeen County Council asked the Local Government Board to fix an official standard for whisky, a standard laying down, for example, the minimum proportion of malt whisky in a blend. Another serious suggestion made was that blends should carry labels bearing the words 'Malts and Grains' and describing the proportions of the whiskies in the blend.

The only possible court of appeal for the grain-whisky distillers from the Fordham decision was to Quarter Sessions at Clerkenwell, London. However unsatisfactory a court for so highly technical a case, it was the only alternative to accepting the North London Police Court judgement. Quarter Sessions, then, began hearing the appeal on 28 May 1906, under the chairmanship of Mr W. R. M'Connell, KC, along with a bench of lay magistrates.

Once more, as at Islington, there was a galaxy of legal and technical talent employed by both sides. The court sat for seven sittings, and the result was a draw, a stalemate: on 25 June chairman M'Connell said no decision could be given as the Bench was equally divided. That also meant that the North London decision still stood as the only legal finding, but not having been confirmed by the court of appeal it had lost a large part of its force. The case could not go to any higher tribunal; the appellants—the former defendants— could apply again for a fresh hearing before a second bench of magistrates at Quarter Sessions, but neither side felt they could trust themselves again to such a mixed tribunal.

Legally, patent-still spirit was not whisky; a blend of patent-still spirit and pot-still whisky was not whisky, was 'not of the nature, substance and quality demanded' when Scotch, or Irish, whisky was requested. Lesser prosecutions occurred here and there, and again at Islington. Deputations waited on John Burns, the first Labour MP to get cabinet rank, who was president of the Local Government Board. But blends continued to be sold, while The DCL widely advertised and sold Cambus single-grain whisky from the distillery of that name. Islington ratepayers were beginning to mutter at the expense of all this, and there came a change in the party structure of the council. A joint deputation of the whisky trade and Islington council finally persuaded Burns to obtain the government's consent to a royal commission 'on whiskey and other potable spirits'. Or, as it was quickly known, the 'What is whisky? commission'. It was a distinguished commission of seven members and secretary under the chairmanship of Lord James of Hereford, an experienced and celebrated lawyer, getting on in years but as shrewd and discerning as ever.

The commission's first sitting, in London, was on 2 March 1908, after which they held thirty-seven sittings to take evidence, examined 116 witnesses, considered various documents, while between sittings some commissioners visited distilleries in Scotland, Ireland and France.

The commission acted promptly, however delayed had been its inception, and on 24 June 1908 issued an interim report. The conclusions in that report basically settled the matter, and were:

1. That no restrictions should be placed upon the processes of, or apparatus used in, the distillation of any spirit to which the term 'whiskey' may be applied as a trade description.

2. That the term 'whiskey' having been recognised in the past as

146

WHAT IS WHISKY?

LORD JAMES OF HEREFORD (*Chairman of the Royal Commission on Whisky*):—

"BE THOU A SPIRIT OF HEALTH OR GOBLIN DAMN'D...
THOU COM'ST IN SUCH A QUESTIONABLE SHAPE
ＴＨＡＴ Ｉ ＷＩＬＬ ＳＰＥＡＫ ＴＯ ＴＨＥＥ." *Hamlet, Act I, Sc. 4.*

applicable to a potable spirit manufactured from (1) malt, or (2) malt and unmalted barley or other cereals, the application of the term 'whiskey' should not be denied to the product manufactured from such materials.

We reserve for further consideration the question of the advisability or otherwise of attaching special significance to particular designations such as 'Scotch Whiskey', 'Irish Whiskey', 'Grain Whiskey', and 'Malt Whiskey''; of placing restrictions upon the use of such designations as trade descriptions to be used in connection with the sale of whiskey.

By the time of that interim report, the commission had held twenty-two sittings, examined seventy-four witnesses, and visited some distilleries, so it is obvious that very little may be quoted here. But these choice few examples are given. Mr (later Sir) Arthur Tedder, chief commissioner of excise and father of the late Lord Tedder, Marshal of the Royal Air Force and of World War II fame, was the first witness called. After much detailed statistical evidence, the following exchange took place:

DR HAROLD BROWN: What is the distinctive character of pot still and patent still whiskey which you regard as being different in character?—Well, I do not think there is any question about this distinction. I should have no difficulty in saying which was which.

CHAIRMAN: Do you think that if a member of the public got a bottle of whiskey containing 80 per cent of pot still and another of 6 per cent, he could tell the difference?—I believe a whiskey drinker could. He would do so by the flavour and aroma.

Then there is a uniform flavour of pot still whiskey?—No. Each distillery produces whiskey of a distinctive flavour. There is a pot still flavour in all of them and yet they may all differ.

How would you describe the difference between pot and patent still whiskey?—I am afraid we are now getting into touch with metaphysics.

Or Tedder on yeast production, which was to play such an important part in winning World War I: 'Yeast making in patent-still distilleries is now a very important industry... Where yeast is manufactured freely for sale, more attention is paid to its production than to the production of spirits.'

The same applied to fusel oil: 'This has become a valuable

148

bye-product; indeed, more so than spirits. I think the great use made of it is for solvent purposes and for varnishes.' (As it turned out, another presage of its value in World War I.)

Mr William H. Ross, managing director of The DCL for the previous eight years, who became chairman of the enlarged DCL in 1925, is our next most important and quoteable witness. He gave this succinct account of the development of blending Scotch:

> Before 1860 the very little blending carried on had to be done after the spirits had paid duty. Irish whiskey at this time was predominant in the market, chiefly on account of its uniformity in style, whereas in Scotland, even amongst pot still whiskies, they were vastly dissimilar. When a man asked for Scotch whisky or spirits, he never knew whether he would get the high flavoured North country, Islay or Campbeltown whiskey, or the less flavoured Lowland malt whiskey, or the pure grain whiskey, patent still.
>
> This was the blender's opportunity, and he soon began to mix the various grades of Scotch whiskey together, and produced a fairly uniform type of whiskey, with none of the pronounced flavours of the individual parts. The public at once took to this new style of whiskey, which they preferred to the stronger flavoured Irish pot whiskey to which they had been accustomed. The popularity of Scotch whiskey in England was due entirely to blended whiskey, which was much better suited to those living a sedentary life.

Ross also made this important point, one on which many malt-whisky distillers agreed with him: 'The Scotch malt distillers have benefited by the growth of blended whiskies, and have participated to some extent with the patent still distillers in the increase which has taken place.'

Finally, Mr (later Sir) Alexander Walker, joint managing director of John Walker & Sons, who gave his own personal views: 'I think that Scotch whiskey, in order to entitle it to that name, should have a high proportion of pot still malt whiskey as its basis . . . I believe the characteristics of Scotch whiskey are entirely got in the pot still. The character of Scotch whiskey as known is only got in the pot still.' To this

149

end Walker proposed that any blend should contain at least 50 per cent malt whisky, and on the subject of blending declared:

> I attribute the necessity for blending, in the first instance, to the fact that it is impossible to make whiskey in a pot still without getting much too great a flavour. You cannot reduce the flavour sufficiently to be sold *per se*. The grain whiskey, which can be made with a very small proportion of secondary products, may be admixed in order to bring down the flavour to a certain extent and keep it within popular taste. That, of course, has gone on increasing as the popular taste has gone to lighter articles.

The alleged modern craze for 'light' whiskies and other spirits is far from being a new, up-to-date fashion!

There we must leave this fascinating stack of evidence, written and spoken, and come to the findings of the commission. The full and final report was issued on 28 July 1909 in a 27-page document, and after what can only be described as a masterly analysis of the evidence the commission stated: 'Finally, we have received no evidence to show that the form of the still has any necessary relation to the wholesomeness of the spirit produced.

'For these reasons we are unable to recommend that the use of the word "whiskey" should be restricted to spirit manufactured by the pot-still process.'

The patent still was thereby legitimised. Then came the real heart of the report, which has, with necessary additions, been incorporated into statute law of the UK:

> Our general conclusion, therefore, on this part of our inquiry is that 'whiskey' is a spirit obtained by distillation from a mash of cereal grains saccharified by the diastase of malt; that 'Scotch whiskey' is whiskey, as above defined, distilled in Scotland; and that 'Irish whiskey' is whiskey, as above defined, distilled in Ireland.

(The whole of Ireland was then, of course, part of the United Kingdom of Great Britain and Ireland.)

As to some suggestions made by witnesses that it was possible to use bad materials, particularly with the patent still, and distillers should state materials used, the report was most emphatic, in a way which would not be encountered today:

> After a full consideration, we report that it is not desirable to require that such declaration should be made.
>
> Interference with trade by the State either by legislation or administration must be justified by its necessity arising from the existence of some evil which, in the interests of the public, requires to be prevented . . .
>
> But, when searching for reasons why special legislation should be applied to whiskey, we had difficulty in finding them. In the numerous distilleries existing in the United Kingdom the trade in whiskey seems to be honestly and fairly conducted. No frauds or semi-frauds were alleged to have been practised.

As to enforcing a minimum age before Scotch was released to the public, the commission made history and rejected the necessity in these words:

> If compulsory bonding is considered as a means of securing the maturity and flavour, as distinct from the wholesomeness, of spirits, it must be borne in mind that spirits of different character do not mature with equal rapidity. A very much longer period is required for the maturation of a heavy pot-still malt whiskey, for example, than for a light patent-still whiskey. Even in the case of spirits of the same character, differences in the condition of storage, such as the nature and size of the vessel in which the spirit is kept, the relative humidity of the place in which it is stored and climatic conditions generally, have a considerable effect in determining the rapidity of maturation. Whatever period might be fixed would inevitably be open to one of two objections; it would either impose an unnecessary burden on particular classes of spirits, or it would be too short for the maturing of other classes . . .

That freedom from compulsory bonding—imprisonment, if you will—was to be an early victim of World War I. But the central core of the report, defining Scotch and Irish as geographical products, is a high-water mark of freedom in British whisky distilling: it left open the type of still, and referred simply to distillation; it did not detail grains to be

used, but spoke only of 'cereals'. If it did insist on saccharifi-
cation by malt, that only confirmed better and traditional
practice and outlawed, without naming it, sulphuric acid as
a conversion agent of the starch in the maize into saccharine
material. Again, freedom was left to mature or not to mature.

Above all, of course, it legitimised the patent still, its
product as a form of whisky, and blending as a permissible
practice. It assured the future of the Scotch whisky industry;
had the report gone the other way, barring revolutions Scotch
would have remained a quaint, limited, provincial—if not,
indeed, parochial—drink patronised by visiting tourists in
the cities and burghs of Scotland, and possibly adopted as a
snob-value curiosity in a few world centres.

It was the green light for expansion; for long-term expansion, that is. In the previous April Lloyd George as Chancellor of the Exchequer had upped the tax on Scotch by 34 per
cent, from 11s the proof gallon to 14s 9d. It took a whole year
to get that budget passed, and although there was a lot of
Scotch sniping on the sidelines, it was Irish whiskey that was
more powerful in getting the budget through: the Irish
Nationalist MPs finally agreed to let the budget through,
with its extra whisky tax, in return for a promise of Home
Rule for Ireland.

Lloyd George, the 'Welsh Goat', as he was nicknamed in
Westminster and Whitehall, was one of the most controversial
figures of the British political scene in the first half of this
century. In his 1915 budget he proposed to double the tax
on spirits, quadruple the tax on wines and do much the same
to beer. As to spirits, in the muddled preliminaries to that
budget, he was disuaded by Mr (later Lord) James Stevenson,
joint managing director of John Walker & Sons, who was
giving his services free to the nation at the time, to drop the
extra tax and instead impose a compulsory minimum age of
three years' maturity before Scotch and various other spirits
could be sold to the British public. A twelve-month interreg-

num was allowed, on payment of extra tax, to Scotch of two years' maturity.

Australia and Canada had led the way well before World War I in insisting on a minimum age or maturity for whisky, but it was only with the passing of the Immature Spirits (Restriction) Act in the spring of 1915 that a three years' minimum age was made compulsory in Great Britain in the case of sales of Scotch to the public.

As Lloyd George put it in his *War Memoirs*:

> In my speech on the 29th April I had said that I intended to impose a graded surtax on the heavier beers, to quadruple the tax on wines, to double the taxes on spirits, and to raise the maximum permissible dilution of spirits from 25 per cent to 36 per cent under proof.
>
> These proposals roused considerable opposition both in and out of the House of Commons. The Irish Party was particularly angry in view of the big brewing and distilling interests in that country. One by one I was compelled to abandon, for the time being, these proposed taxes, and could only retain one insignificant but quite useful little restriction in the shape of a prohibition on the sale of spirits less than three years old, the object being to prohibit the newer and more fiery spirit. Even round this a fierce controversy arose between the rival distilling interests—the 'Pot versus Patent' fight—for manufacturers of pot-still whisky made a practice of keeping their product several years to mature, whereas the output of the patent still was marketed straight away.

Here Lloyd George is guilty of one of his frequent inaccuracies: at the time of the 'What is whisky?' proceedings, The DCL had marketed Cambus grain whisky as a single whisky and with an age of seven years. While some blenders may have used young, immature grain whisky the better firms still with us today invariably used only mature malt and grain whiskies in their blends.

But it is quite a thought that the British minimum age, of three years, for retailing Scotch arose from a wartime emergency measure to save the face of the Chancellor of the

Exchequer in having to abandon his proposed extra taxes on alcoholic beverages. Further, that it arose due to the personal influence and persuasiveness of one man, James Stevenson, of John Walker & Sons, who then and until his death rendered invaluable national service without thought of reward.

That minimum age requirement is a major landmark in the world development of Scotch, and had many ramifications in the trade. Many firms sold out at vastly increased prices for their mature whiskies—which had been in slump conditions —and this in turn led The DCL to take a larger and more permanent interest in both malt-whisky distilling and blending. Big firms with big stocks to fall back on became even bigger; small men who bought largely from week to week as they needed supplies for blending ceased. Northern Irish distilleries and blenders, who so largely depended on sales of what were now immature whiskey, suffered badly, and their extinction could be foreseen. In brief, while that Immature Act caused a minor revolution insofar as it affected the public, it caused a major revolution within the industry.

Lloyd George became Minister of Munitions and was succeeded as Chancellor by M'Kenna, who had to introduce an autumn budget. He and the previous chancellor had been irritated since 1909 by distillers and others anticipating extra taxes on their goods by making heavy taxpaid withdrawals of spirits from bond ahead of their budgets. So, in the tradition of his 'master' and in line with the latter's opposition to—if not hatred of—the trade, M'Kenna issued instructions in September, ahead of his budget, limiting taxpaid withdrawals from bond to the daily average of the previous three months, and then to the daily average of the last six or twelve months. It was a revolutionary taxation procedure, and M'Kenna himself admitted the instructions were illegal. Like so many practices which begin as illegal it has now been granted a place in British law, but it remains an unjust infringement of the rights of the individual trader to do what he wishes and judges best with his own property. As always, the first victims of any war are truth and liberty. M'Kenna got away with it, and national stamina has sunk so low that it has been incorporated in the law of Great Britain as a matter of course and without any serious opposition. A minor revolution again, maybe, but one where Scotch whisky has again influenced, if not changed, the course of British constitutional history.

Apart from three successive years' tax increases on Scotch —in the 1918, 1919 and 1920 budgets—which multiplied almost five times the pre-war tax on Scotch from 14s 9d ($1.80) the proof gallon to 72s 6d ($8.70) and so deliberately restricted the citizen consumer's freedom of choice, and apart from minor skirmishes between Scotch and government, Scotch did not move on to the legal scene again until the budget of 1933.

Year after year industry leaders had tried, unsuccessfully, to persuade the chancellor to lower the tax on Scotch, especially in the darkest years of the world depression when the whole industry was faced with ruin. Now the royal commission of 1908-9 had defined Scotch whisky. As with all governments, the report was noted and filed, tucked away in the never-never land of bureaucracy. The 1915 Immature Spirits Act had imposed a minimum age on Scotch as sold to the British public.

The chancellor during all these years refused to listen to the pleas of the hard-pressed industry, but as a sop Neville Chamberlain, the Chancellor of the Exchequer, included in his Finance Bill (later the Finance Act, 1933), the first-ever legal definition of Scotch in Section 34 of the act. It had, of course, the limitation of being only in a Finance Act for one year and related only to the description of Scotch in official certificates and permits as issued by Customs and Excise. The section was, however, something of a landmark, however belated, in the Scotch story and paved the way for a proper statutory definition almost twenty years later. It was, in effect, a combination of the 1909 royal commission definition and the 1915 Immature Act, and read:

> For the purpose of sub-section (9) of Section 105 of the Spirits Act, 1880 (which relates to the accuracy of the spirits in a permit or certificate), Spirits described as Scotch Whisky shall not be deemed to correspond to that description unless they have been obtained by distillation in Scotland from a mash of cereal grains saccharified by the diastase of malt and have been matured in a bonded warehouse in casks for a period of at least three years.

It was a curious and in some ways deficient definition: the plural 'casks' opened possibilities of interminable legal wrangles; bonded warehouses at distilleries were then few and far between; and the description related only to permits and certificates. But it was, at least, a move in the right direction, however tardy.

Towards the end of 1938 arose several cases in Scotland under the Merchandise Marks Act in which firms were charged with selling as Scotch whisky a whisky which was not in fact Scotch whisky, but a mixture of Scotch and Northern Irish whisky. These cases constitute a most important landmark in the history of Scotch, as the courts laid down that only whisky which is entirely distilled in Scotland has the right to bear the name of Scotch. It was a decision described at the time as 'of supreme importance to the Scotch whisky trade'.

We need not enter into the minutiae of the cases, which began at the Glasgow Sheriff Court in December 1938. It was alleged that the firms sold whiskies as Scotch which were mixtures of Scotch and Northern Irish whiskies, the proportions in different cases being of the order of 51 per cent Scotch and 49 per cent Northern Irish, 70 per cent and 30 per cent, 77 per cent and 23 per cent, 38 per cent and 62 per cent Scotch and Northern Irish respectively. In all, eight firms were involved.

On 30 January 1939, after lengthy legal and technical argu-

156

ment, Sheriff Guild gave a learned judgement towards the
end of which he said:

> In the first place, I do not see that I have to frame a definition
> of Scotch whisky. As I see it, the question I have to decide is a
> much narrower question, namely, whether the content of the
> term Scotch whisky as that term falls to be construed for the
> purposes of the Merchandise Marks Act there is of necessity im-
> plied the representation that the whole contents of the bottle,
> in so far as these are technically or popularly described as whisky,
> must be the produce of Scotland.
>
> The next question is what is the effect of the Finance Act of
> 1933. As I read the section the definition therein incorporated
> is imported for limited purposes and for those alone.
>
> I do not think that it can reasonably be held to go further
> than regulating the procedure in regard to certain documents
> required by the Excise regulations. This leaves what one may
> term the general question. The term 'Scotch' is ambiguous, it
> may import the country of origin, or it may be a label denoting
> a set of well-recognised characteristics.

Lamenting that 'all the authorities are English', the sheriff
discussed them and summed up:

> Now as far as I can see I have to choose between the two view-
> points. As the case of Lemy v. Watson is the most recent exposi-
> tion of a Court of high authority of this difficult Act I think I
> am bound to follow it. It would seem that in the ratio of that
> case where a term on a label is ambiguous there should be at
> least some evidence that the usage under challenge was known
> to the consuming public. I do not see any such evidence here.
> From that it follows there must be a conviction.

That is, it was an offence at law to sell as Scotch whisky a
whisky which was not entirely Scottish in origin; that the
term 'Scotch' is geographic in connotation. It is not just like
the old phrases of 'Irish stew' or 'Brighton rock', which can
be made anywhere around the world and still carry those
names. Scotch whisky, it was ruled, could only be made in
Scotland.

Of course there was an appeal. The Justiciary Appeal
Court in Edinburgh upheld Sheriff Guild in the test case,

declaring that he was entitled to convict. To quote a reliable report of the time: 'The Lord Justice-General said that it seemed that the Scotch whisky which the appellants used for their blending was Scotch pot still whisky, and that the Irish whiskey which was used was Irish patent still whiskey. The Sheriff's finding, as his Lordship construed it, was substantially that when whisky was sold as Scotch whisky, the representation that it was Scotch whisky carried the meaning that the entire contents of the container in which it was sold were distilled in Scotland.' The sheriff had come to that conclusion by the evidence.

Again: 'On that evidence it was idle to suggest that the Sheriff was disentitled to come to the conclusion at which he did and to hold that Scotch whisky meant whisky which was in its entirety distilled in Scotland.' Finally: 'In his Lordship's opinion there was no evidence as found by the Sheriff to force him to come to a conclusion opposite to that which he did come, and that the conclusion at which he arrived was fully supported by the evidence.'

Scotch whisky can only be made in Scotland. A few later cases followed that year, but World War II intervened before there could be any governmental intervention to clarify the law. Meanwhile, year after year industry leaders pleaded that the law be amended in line with the decision of the courts. At length that war ended, and as part of the postwar rehabilitation and reconstruction, legislation concerning Customs and Excise and matters coming under them were consolidated into the Customs and Excise Act of 1952, one clause of which, Clause 243 (I) (b), reads: 'Spirits described as Scotch whisky shall not be deemed to correspond to that description unless they have been obtained by distillation in Scotland from a mash of cereal grains saccharified by the diastase of malt and have been matured in warehouse in cask for a period of at least three years.' Notice that it drops the plural 'casks', while at the same time it omits the word 'bonded' before warehouse.

Otherwise its parentage and descent are as outlined earlier in considering the Finance Act of 1933.

This definition in the statute law has been invaluable, not only at home but also abroad, in fighting cases of spurious, bogus Scotch—a matter in which The Scotch Whisky Association is engaged year in, year out, maintaining a constant and worldwide consumer protection service in order that the lover of Scotch receives what he asks for; that he is given, in the old phrase, an article 'of the nature, substance and quality demanded'. It serves also, of course, to protect that valuable national asset which is Scotch whisky, one of the major visible exports of the country, and still the largest single dollar-earning export.

True, British law is not accepted and administered as law in every foreign country where Scotch may have to be protected, but, without entering into a long legal dissertation on the subject, British law may be quoted as above and local laws brought into force.

It is only since about 1959 or 1960 that this world vigilance has become so important, particularly with the export of sizeable quantities of immature 'whisky'—spirit, that is, which would have become entitled to the name of Scotch whisky when mature—and the still increasing quantities of malt whisky from Scotland used for mixing with locally made spirit and too often 'dressed up', with tartan packaging, Scottish names, etc, to retail in non-English-speaking markets as Scotch.

Because of the growing trade in exports of immature whisky as the 1950s drew to a close, the Finance Act of 1960, acting in defence of Scotch as an important national asset and foreign currency earner, specifically applied the 1952 Customs and Excise Act definition of Scotch as quoted above to exports of spirits. This meant that immature 'whisky' could not be described as 'Scotch whisky' when shipped abroad but would go as 'immature British plain cereal spirits'. (The main

159

market for them is Sweden, where the State Monopoly imports them to mature in Sweden before sale to the public.)

A further and more detailed description was given to Scotch in the Finance Act of 1969, which also fits in with the American definition of whiskey, by which, for example, spirits distilled above 190° proof on the US scale of alcoholic strength are neutral spirits.

The relevant schedule of the 1969 Finance Act reads:

1. In relation to spirits distilled on or after 1st August, 1969, Section 243 (I) (b) of the Customs and Excise Act 1952 (which defines Scotch whisky) shall cease to have effect, and for all purposes of customs and excise—
    (a) the expression 'whisky' shall mean spirits which have been distilled from a mash of cereals which has been—
      (i) saccharified by the diastase of malt contained therein with or without other natural diastases approved for the purpose by the Commissioners; and
      (ii) fermented by the action of yeast; and
      (iii) distilled at less than 166.4 degrees proof in such a way that the distillate has an aroma and flavour derived from the materials used, and which have been matured in wooden casks in warehouse for a period of at least three years;
    (b) the expression 'Scotch whisky' shall mean whisky which has been distilled in Scotland;
    (c) the expression 'blended whisky' or 'blended Scotch whisky' shall mean a blend of a number of distillates each of which separately is entitled to the description whisky or Scotch whisky as the case may be;
    (d) the period for which any blended whisky or blended Scotch whisky shall be treated as having been matured as mentioned in sub-paragraph (a) of this paragraph shall be taken to be that applicable in the case of the most recently distilled of the spirits contained in the blend.

We may note that 166.4 proof on the British scale corresponds to 190 proof on the US scale, and as malt whisky is always distilled at much less strength than this—usually averaging 125 proof, or 25 over proof—the 166.4 proof maximum above is a safeguard that the charge cannot be brought against Scotch grain whisky as made in the patent still of being neutral spirit. It never is neutral, though of less distinguished and individual character than pot-still malt whiskies; but over the years there have been accusations from parts of the American distilling world that Scotch grain is 'only neutral spirit', an accusation made to decry the Scotch blends. The foregoing Finance Act definition, and excise supervision of distilling, make that charge false and untenable.

Such has been the fate of Scotch whisky in its legal development, as distinct from the unhappy fate that has befallen it in its taxation tangle. From that early, 1890-91 select committee inquiry into its blending and bonding, which acquitted it, it passed next to the great 'What is whisky?' inquiry by a royal commission, to emerge with both major sectors clarified and authorised. From the trials of World War I it emerged with the established trade's practice of maturing made compulsory by law, and from the throes of the Great Depression it won its first legal definition, a definition made statutory in 1952 and further detailed as late as 1969.

Who could have foretold when Friar John Cor was granted his eight bolls of malt in 1494 to make aqua vitae, when Besse Campbell was ordered to cease making it some fifty years later, that the native spirit of Scotland, the fruit of the land's four elements as organised by the native Scots, would engage in such detail the attention of the Mother of Parliaments?

But such has been the destiny of Scotch whisky in its world progress to become the premier potable spirit of the globe.

Appendix 1

Distillery	Advice	Proprietor
Ardmore, Kennethmont, Aberdeenshire. Tel: Kennethmont 213	Ring for appointment if possible	Wm Teacher & Sons Ltd Glasgow
Blair Atholl, Pitlochry, Perthshire. Tel: Pitlochry 161	Closed mid-July to mid-September. Rest of year: Monday, Wednesday and Friday, 3 pm	Arthur Bell & Sons Ltd Perth
Dalmore, Alness, Ross-shire.	Notice for large parties. Weekdays: 10-12 2.30-4.30	Mackenzie Bros Dalmore Ltd Alness
Fettercairn, Fettercairn, Kincardinshire. Tel: Fettercairn 244	Notify Mr J. S. Livie	Fettercairn Distillery Ltd Fettercairn
Girvan Grain Distillery, Girvan, Ayrshire. Tel: Girvan 3091	Monday-Friday. No appointment necessary	Wm Grant & Sons Ltd Glasgow
Glendronach, Huntly, Aberdeenshire. Tel: Forgue 202	Ring for appointment if possible	Wm Teacher & Sons Ltd Glasgow
Glenfiddich, Dufftown, Banffshire. Tel: Dufftown 375	Monday-Friday. No appointment necessary	Wm Grant & Sons Ltd Glasgow

163

Distillery	Advice	Proprietor
Glengoyne, Dumgoyne, Stirlingshire. Tel: Killearn 254	Notify the manager	Robertson & Baxter Ltd Glasgow
Glen Grant-Glenlivet, Rothes, Morayshire. Tel: Rothes 243	By appointment. Ring distillery direct	J. & J. Grant Glen Grant Ltd Rothes
Glen Mhor and Glen, Albyn Distilleries, Inverness.	Mid-June to mid-September. 9.30 am-4.30 pm	The Distillers Co Ltd Edinburgh
Glenugie, Peterhead, Aberdeenshire. Tel: Peterhead 110	Notice for large parties	Long John International Ltd Glasgow
Ladyburn, Girvan, Ayrshire. Tel: Girvan 3091	Monday-Friday	Wm Grant & Sons Ltd Glasgow
Laphroaig, Port Ellen, Isle of Islay, Argyllshire. Tel: Port Ellen 18	Notify Mr J. McDougal at distillery	Long John Distilleries Glasgow
Macallan, Craigellachie, Banffshire. Tel: Aberlour 350	By appointment: Mr Harbinson Mornings: Monday and Tuesday Afternoons: Thursday and Friday	Macallan-Glenlivet Ltd Craigellachie
Strathmill, Keith, Banffshire. Tel: Keith 2531	By appointment Afternoons	International Distiller & Vintners Ltd London
Tormore, Advie, Grantown-on-Spey, Morayshire. Tel: Advie 232	Notice for large parties	Long John International Ltd Glasgow

164

Distillery	*Advice*	*Proprietor*
Tullibardine,	Monday afternoon	Brodie Hepburn
Blackford,	Tuesday morning	Ltd
Perthshire.		Glasgow
Tel: Blackford 252		

(On authority of The Scotch Whisky Association)

Appendix 2

Distillery	*Parent company*	*Location*
Grain		
Ben Nevis	Ben Nevis Distillery (Fort William) Ltd	Fort William
Caledonian	DCL	Edinburgh
Cambus	DCL	Cambus
Cameronbridge	DCL	Windygates
Carsebridge	DCL	Alloa
Dumbarton	Hiram Walker–Gooderham & Worts Ltd	Dumbarton
Garnheath	Publicker Industries Inc	Airdrie
Girvan	Wm Grant & Sons Ltd	Girvan
Invergordon	Invergordon Distillers (Holdings) Ltd	Invergordon
Lochside	Macnab Distilleries Ltd	Montrose
North British	North British Distillery Co Ltd	Edinburgh
Port Dundas	DCL	Glasgow
Strathclyde	Long John International Ltd	Glasgow
Strathmore	North of Scotland Distilling Co Ltd	Cambus
Lowland malt		
Auchentoshan	Eadie Cairn & Co	Dalmuir
Bladnoch	Bladnoch Distillery Ltd	Wigtown
Glenkinchie	DCL	East Lothian
Inverleven	Hiram Walker–Gooderham & Worts Ltd	Dumbarton
Kinclaith	Long John International Ltd	Glasgow
Ladyburn	Wm Grant & Sons Ltd	Girvan
Littlemill	Barton Distilling (Scotland) Ltd	Bowling
Lomond	Hiram Walker–Gooderham & Worts Ltd	Dumbarton
Moffat	Publicker Industries Inc	Airdrie
Rosebank	DCL	Falkirk
St Magdalene	DCL	Linlithgow
Islay malt		
Ardbeg	Ardbeg Distillery Trust (72½%)	Islay
	DCL (15%)	
	Hiram Walker (Scotland) (12½%)	

167

Distillery	Parent company	Location
Bowmore	Sherriff's Bowmore Distillery Ltd	Islay
Bruichladdich	Invergordon Distillers (Holdings) Ltd	Islay
Bunnahabhain	Highland Distilleries Co Ltd	Islay
Caol Ila	DCL	Islay
Lagavulin	DCL	Islay
Laphroaig	Long John International Ltd	Islay
Port Ellen	DCL	Islay

Campbeltown malt

Glen Scotia	Amalgamated Distilled Products Ltd	Campbeltown
Springbank	J. & A. Mitchell & Co Ltd	Campbeltown

Highland malt

Aberfeldy	DCL	Aberfeldy
Aberlour–Glenlivet	Aberlour–Glenlivet Distillery Co Ltd	Aberlour
Ardmore	Teachers (Distillers) Ltd	Kennethmont
Aultmore–Glenlivet	DCL	Keith
Balblair	Hiram Walker–Gooderham & Worts Ltd	Edderton
Balmenach–Glenlivet	DCL	Cromdale
Balvenie	Wm Grant & Sons Ltd	Dufftown
Banff	DCL	Banff
Ben Nevis	Ben Nevis Distillery (Fort William) Ltd	Fort William
Benriach–Glenlivet	Glenlivet Distillers Ltd	Elgin
Benrinnes	DCL	Aberlour
Benromach–Glenlivet	DCL	Forres
Ben Wyvis	Invergordon Distillers (Holdings) Ltd	Invergordon
Blair Athol	Arthur Bell & Sons Ltd	Pitlochry
Caperdonich	Glenlivet Distillers Ltd	Rothes
Cardow	DCL	Cardow
Clynelish	DCL	Brora
Coleburn–Glenlivet	DCL	Elgin
Convalmore–Glenlivet	DCL	Dufftown
Cragganmore–Glenlivet	DCL	Ballindalloch
Craigellachie–Glenlivet	DCL	Craigellachie

Distillery	Parent company	Location
Dailuaine–Glenlivet	DCL	Carron
Dallus Dhu	DCL	Forres
Dalmore	Dalmore, Whyte & Mackay Ltd	Alness
Dalwhinnie	DCL	Dalwhinnie
Deanston	Invergordon Distillers (Holdings) Ltd	Doune
Dufftown–Glenlivet	Arthur Bell & Sons Ltd	Dufftown
Edradour	Wm Whiteley & Co	Pitlochry
Fettercairn	Tomintoul–Glenlivet Distillery Ltd	Fettercairn
Glen Albyn	DCL	Inverness
Glenallachie	Scottish & Newcastle Breweries Ltd	Aberlour
Glenburgie–Glenlivet	Hiram Walker (Scotland) Ltd	Forres
Glencadam	Hiram Walker (Scotland) Ltd	Brechin
Glendronach	Teacher (Distillers) Ltd	Huntly
Glendullan–Glenlivet	DCL	Dufftown
Glen Elgin–Glenlivet	DCL	Elgin
Glenfarclas–Glenlivet	J. & G. Grant	Ballindalloch
Glenfiddich	Wm Grant & Sons Ltd	Dufftown
Glengarioch	Stanley P. Morrison Ltd	Old Meldrum
Glenglassaugh	Highland Distilleries Co Ltd	Portsoy
Glengoyne	Robertson & Baxter Ltd	Killearn
Glen Grant–Glenlivet	Glenlivet Distillers Ltd	Rothes
Glen Keith–Glenlivet	Distillers Corp–Seagrams	Keith
Glenlivet, The	Glenlivet Distillers Ltd	Glenlivet
Glenlochy	DCL	Fort William
Glenlossie–Glenlivet	DCL	Elgin
Glen Mhor	DCL	Inverness
Glenmorangie	MacDonald Martin Distilleries Ltd	Tain
Glen Moray–Glenlivet	MacDonald Martin Distilleries Ltd	Elgin
Glenrothes–Glenlivet	Highland Distilleries Co Ltd	Rothes
Glen Spey	International Distillers & Vintners Ltd	Rothes
Glentauchers–Glenlivet	DCL	Keith
Glenturret	Glenturret Distillery Ltd	Crieff

169

Distillery	Parent company	Location
Glenugie	Long John International Ltd	Peterhead
Glenury-Royal	DCL	Stonehaven
Highland Park	Highland Distilleries Co Ltd	Orkney
Hillside	DCL	Montrose
Imperial–Glenlivet	DCL	Carron
Inchgower	Arthur Bell & Sons Ltd	Buckie
Isle of Jura	Scottish & Newcastle Breweries Ltd (72.69%)	Isle of Jura
Knockando	International Distillers & Vintners Ltd	Cardow
Knockdhu	DCL	Banffshire
Ledaig	Ledaig Distillery (Tobermory) Ltd	Tobermory
Linkwood–Glenlivet	DCL	Elgin
Loch Lomond	Barton Distilling (Scotland) Ltd	Alexandria
Lochside	Macnab Distilleries Ltd	Montrose
Longmorn–Glenlivet	Glenlivet Distillers Ltd	Elgin
Macallan–Glenlivet	Macallan–Glenlivet Ltd	Craigellachie
Macduff	Block, Grey & Block	Banff
Mannochmore	DCL	Elgin
Millburn	DCL	Inverness
Miltonduff–Glenlivet	Hiram Walker (Scotland) Ltd	Elgin
Mortlach	DCL	Dufftown
North Port	DCL	Brechin
Oban	DCL	Oban
Ord	DCL	Beauly
Pulteney	Hiram Walker (Scotland) Ltd	Wick
Royal Brackla	DCL	Nairn
Royal Lochnagar	DCL	Balmoral
Scapa	Hiram Walker (Scotland) Ltd	Kirkwall
Speyburn–Glenlivet	DCL	Rothes
Strathisla–Glenlivet	Distillers Corp–Seagrams	Keith
Strathmill	International Distillers & Vintners Ltd	Keith
Talisker	DCL	Isle of Skye
Tamdhu–Glenlivet	Highland Distilleries Co Ltd	Knockando
Tamnavulin–Glenlivet	Invergordon Distillers (Holdings) Ltd	Tomnavulin

Distillery	Parent company	Location
Teaninich	DCL	Tomatin
Tomatin	Tomatin Distillers Co Ltd	Alness
Tomintoul–Glenlivet	The Tomintoul–Glenlivet Distillery Ltd	Ballindalloch
Tormore	Long John International Ltd	Advie
Tullibardine	Invergordon Distillers (Holdings) Ltd	Blackford

To the foregoing should be added Highland Malt Distilleries planned or under construction at the time of writing:

Auchroisk	International Distillers & Vintners Ltd	Mulben
In the Braes of Glenlivet	Distillers Corp–Seagrams	Banffshire

Appendix 3

SCOTCH WHISKY PRODUCTION IN THE DISTILLING YEAR ENDING
30 SEPTEMBER IN MILLIONS OF PROOF GALLONS

| Year ending 30 September | Distilleries using | | Total |
	Malt only	Malt and other cereals	
1939	10.7	18.5	29.2
1940	7.2	6.2	13.2
1941	3.2	Nil	3.2
1942	3.2	Nil	3.2
1943	Nil	Nil	Nil
1944	Nil	Nil	Nil
1945	3.7	5.0	8.7
1946	5.8	8.5	14.3
1947	3.5	5.6	9.1
1948	8.3	12.5	20.8
1949	11.3	16.3	27.6
1950	12.7	16.4	29.1
1951	12.2	14.8	27.0
1952	12.6	17.4	30.0
1953	12.3	13.9	26.2
1954	13.7	19.1	32.8
1955	15.1	25.3	40.4
1956	15.9	27.1	43.0
1957	18.2	31.4	49.6
1958	20.6	33.7	54.3
1959	22.4	36.6	59.0
1960	25.1	44.6	69.7
1961	26.5	49.4	75.9
1962	27.1	57.0	84.1
1963	28.9	65.2	94.1
1964	33.0	82.0	115.0
1965	39.3	95.8	135.1
1966	44.9	97.8	142.7
1967	51.1	74.6	125.7
1968	47.8	65.9	113.7

Year ending 30 September	Distilleries using Malt only	Malt and other cereals	Total
1969	51.4	75.0	126.4
1970	53.8	88.1	141.9
1971	60.3	87.2	147.5
1972	66.1	92.9	159.0

Appendix 4

Year	Gallons
1939	144.25
1940	142.6
1941	129.6
1942	114.0
1943	103.7
1944	92.0
1945	84.8
1946	86.0
1947	79.8
1948	86.7
1949	98.9
1950	111.7
1951	124.1
1952	137.8
1953	145.5
1954	152.9
1955	167.9
1956	179.9
1957	196.5
1958	225.7
1959	245.7
1960	264.8
1961	296.2
1962	325.9
1963	360.7
1964	406.8
1965	468.4
1966	540.2
1967	606.1
1968	657.9
1969	702.4
1970	761.4
1971	814.5
1972	863.4

Appendix 5

Year	Gallons
1939	6.9
1940	Not available
1941	6.2
1942	5.4
1943	6.1
1944	5.8
1945	4.6
1946	4.7
1947	4.7
1948	3.2
1949	2.5
1950	3.0
1951	3.8
1952	3.9
1953	3.9
1954	4.3
1955	4.9
1956	5.4
1957	5.8
1958	6.1

With Scotch supplies for UK consumption freed from quotas and
rations in the spring of 1959 it is more convenient to take UK Scotch
consumption now in millions of proof gallons in the calendar year

Year	Gallons
1959	6.9
1960	7.3
1961	7.9
1962	7.9

177

Year	Gallons
1963	8.7
1964	9.2
1965	9.0
1966	9.0
1967	9.2
1968	9.8
1969	9.3
1970	10.5
1971	11.1
1972	12.5 (estimated)

Appendix 6

SCOTCH WHISKY EXPORTS IN MILLIONS OF PROOF GALLONS AND
VALUE IN MILLIONS OF POUNDS PER CALENDAR YEAR

FIGURES FOR THE USA IN BRACKETS

Year	Gallons	£s
1939	9.4 (4.8)	12.7 (6.985)
1940	11.3 (6.97)	16.2 (10.5)
1941	8.5 (4.969)	13.6 (8.2)
1942	5.5 (3.5)	9.7 (6.2)
1943	5.2 (3.4)	9.3 (6.1)
1944	4.4 (2.6)	8.1 (4.8)
1945	4.7 (2.2)	8.6 (3.9)
1946	5.9 (2.8)	10.9 (5.3)
1947	6.8 (3.99)	13.6 (8.0)
1948	7.9 (4.6)	16.2 (9.5)
1949	8.5 (5.0)	18.7 (11.0)
1950	9.7 (5.8)	23.3 (16.8)
1951	10.6 (6.1)	29.6 (17.9)
1952	11.5 (6.3)	33.0 (18.5)
1953	13.2 (7.2)	37.8 (20.8)
1954	13.7 (7.1)	39.1 (20.8)
1955	15.4 (7.99)	43.6 (23.4)
1956	16.4 (8.7)	47.6 (25.5)
1957	17.9 (9.8)	52.1 (28.6)
1958	19.3 (10.8)	55.9 (31.6)
1959	21.7 (12.1)	61.9 (34.9)
1960	23.1 (12.5)	65.6 (36.0)
1961	26.8 (14.7)	74.4 (40.9)
1962	30.1 (16.3)	80.9 (43.4)
1963	31.8 (16.6)	84.8 (43.9)
1964	35.0 (18.1)	92.3 (46.4)
1965	39.7 (20.5)	107.0 (54.0)
1966	41.6 (22.7)	120.4 (62.9)
1967	43.1 (23.7)	122.4 (64.0)

Year	Gallons	£s
1968	59.2 (33.3)	176.6 (93.4)
1969	52.4 (26.6)	167.5 (81.1)
1970	62.0 (34.4)	194.1 (97.6)
1971	70.3 (35.6)	226.9 (109.3)
1972	68.8 (31.9)	227.9 (101.1)

Index

181

Licensing System rates, 53-5;
nineteenth-century rates, 60;
post-World War I, 155;
World War II and after, 76
et seq, 96 *et seq*

Edinburgh distilleries, 15
Elgood, L. A., 101-2
Enzymes, 16, 63
Eunson, Magnus, 125
Excise officer's description, 41,
117
Exports, value of, 9, 75 *et seq*,
93 *et seq*, 102 *et seq*;
parliamentary praise, 105,
111 *et seq*, 176-7
Exports, volume of, 9, 25, 75
et seq, 93 *et seq*, 102 *et seq*,
111 *et seq*, 176-7

Fergusson, Robert, 45-6, 120-21
Ferintosh distillery, 39, 121
Fermentation, in patent-still
plants, 17; in pot-still plants,
65
Forbes, Bishop, *Journal* of, 41
Forbes, Duncan, 38-9, 122
Forteviot, Lord, 84, 89, 92-3
Funeral, 1618 uiskie, 37, 42-3,
117-18
Fusel oil, 18, 28, 140

Geographic significance, 26-7,
156
Gin, 19, 41
Glasgow, 35
Glasgow distilleries, 15
Glenlivet, The, 57-8, 123
Grain whisky, distillation of,
16 *et seq*; legal battle, 139 *et*

seq; *see also*, Coffey, A., and
Patent still
Grampians, 31, 57
Grant, Elizabeth, of Rothie-
murchus, 131-3
Guardian, Manchester, 85

Haig, near Dublin, 16
Haig, Robert, 1655 distilling,
38
Hard-currency markets, 95,
100, 102
Hebrides, 31, 44, 116
Hereford, Lord James of, 146
Highland Park distillery, 125
Hogg, James, 123
Holinshed, describes Scotch,
35-6
Home consumption of Scotch,
turn of century, 24; 1820 and
1826, 60; around World War
II, 75 *et seq*, 97 *et seq*, 102-3,
112 *et seq*, 174-5

Illicit distilling, 55; numbers,
60
Imperial gallon, 1825, 60
Inverness, 32, 43
Inverness Courier, 130, 134
Irish whiskey, 21, 26, 149
Irvine, 35
Islington Borough Council,
141-2

Jamesons, Dublin, 16
Johnson, Samuel, 43-5, 119
Johnstone, Harcourt, 81

King George IV, 132-4
King James IV, 32

Kintyre, 30
Kirkliston distillery, 13
Knockdhu distillery, 138

Lagavulin distillery, 124
Lancet, 141-2
Licensing System, 49 *et seq*;
    abolished, 56
Lloyd George, 25-6, 28, 153
Lockhart, 133-4

MacGregor, Alasdair Alpine,
    117-18
Maize, in patent-still plant,
    16 *et seq*
Malt whiskies, categories, 61;
    production methods, 63 *et
    seq*
Malt, with patent still, 16 *et
    seq*; with pot still, 62-4
Maturation, 10, 18; made
    compulsory, 27-8; at patent-
    still plants, 18; at pot-still
    plants, 68; royal commission
    on, 151; minimum age, 153-4
Maxwell, Sir Herbert, MP, 141
Methylation Act, 20
Miltonduff–Glenlivet distillery,
    126
Ministers of Food: Morrison,
    76; Col Llewellen, 89-90;
    Lord Woolton, 91; Sir Ben
    Smith, 93; Strachey, 95;
    Webb, 104
Morewood, Samuel, 56, 118-19
Moryson, Fynes, 36

National Association of
    Alcoholic Beverage
    Importers, 77

Netherlands, 31, 120
North of Scotland Malt
    Distillers Association, 138

Off-Licences Association, 142-3

Patent still, 16 *et seq*
Pattison failure, 24
Peat, 10, 11, 63
Perthshire smuggling, 129
Pitt the Younger, taxes, 48-50,
    122
Pot-still distilleries, 12, 18;
    numbers, 61; resume work
    1945, 91
Production of Scotch, 22-3, 24;
    earliest statistics known, 47;
    in nineteenth century, 60-61;
    in and after World War II,
    73 *et seq*, 94 *et seq*; freed,
    108, 112 *et seq*, 171-2
Proof, defined, 106-7
Proof strengths, pot and patent
    stills, 18

Repeal of Prohibition, 74
Ross, Sir Henry J., 95, 99, 101,
    105, 107-8, 109-10, 111
Ross, Wm H., 149
Royal commission, on whisky,
    19; definitions, 26, 146 *et seq*
Royal Lochnagar distillery,
    134-5

Saccharimeter, 58
Sale of Food & Drugs Act, 137
    et seq
Scotch defined, 26, 106, 139-40;
    Fordham's definition, 143-4,
    146-7; 1933 Finance Act,